East Asian Civilizations

THE EDWIN O. REISCHAUER LECTURES, 1986

East Asian Civilizations

A DIALOGUE IN FIVE STAGES

Wm. Theodore de Bary

HARVARD UNIVERSITY PRESS
CAMBRIDGE, MASSACHUSETTS
LONDON, ENGLAND

This book is printed on acid-free paper, and its binding materials
have been chosen for strength and durability.

Library of Congress Cataloging-in-Publication Data

De Bary, William Theodore, 1919–
    East Asian civilizations.

    (The Edwin O. Reischauer lectures; 1986)
    Bibliography: p.
    Includes index.
    1. East Asia—Civilization. I. Title. II. Series.
DS509.3.D43 1988   950   87-14928
ISBN 0-674-22405-1 (alk. paper)

For Donald Keene

Preface

WHEN I CAME TO HARVARD in the fall of 1941 on a traveling fellowship from Columbia, it was my good fortune to have Edwin O. Reischauer as a professor in Elementary Japanese and in a course on the history of Eastern Asia (as his autobiography now describes it, though it was then given in the "Far Eastern" Department). What impressed me about the history course was its breadth and, even more, as I reflect on it today, its cultural depth. With his credentials as a Japan specialist, Reischauer could easily have confined his attention to his own home ground. With his interest in politics and international relations, he could, even on the larger scene of East Asia, have left out anything earlier than the Opium War or Perry's arrival in Japan. That he did otherwise, going back to the beginnings of Chinese civilization and coming down through the successive stages of its development and influence on Japan, explains how it was that in this course I read for the first time such great works as the *Analects* of Confucius and the *Lotus Sūtra*. Any course that opens up such books to you, if it does nothing more, is bound to be memorable. Yet Reischauer did indeed do more; among other things he included within his scope Korea, the so-called Hermit Kingdom, which had long since lost its independence and to which, in those days, hardly anyone else paid much attention. Thus from the start Reischauer was a true East Asianist.

That course was succeeded, I believe, by the better-known Rice Paddies course, the text for which, *East Asia: The Great Tradition*, further embodied Reischauer's broad approach. I was not a witness to this later development, but in my post-war studies at Columbia Ryusaku Tsunoda took the same large view. He was an offspring of the Meiji period, with deep roots in Japan's continental past (if that idea is not too surprising for those who think of Japan as originally and essentially insular), and he confirmed the East Asian consciousness Reischauer had awakened in me. When I gave the first of the four Edwin O. Reischauer Lectures on East Asian Affairs in November 1986, I acknowledged that early debt, and with this book I wish to do something further to carry on what I consider to be a great tradition.

The first four chapters deal with East Asian civilizations in four broad stages: (1) the formative stage (roughly the eleventh century B.C. through the second century A.D.), when classical China developed the basic ideas and institutions that later became part of the classical inheritance of other East Asian peoples; (2) the Buddhist age (the third century through the tenth century), in which the dominant and pervasive cultural force in East Asia was Mahayana Buddhism, with indigenous traditions surviving at a bedrock level; (3) the Neo-Confucian age (the eleventh through the nineteenth century), in which Neo-Confucianism assumed the leading role in new social and cultural activities, while Buddhism struggled for survival on the now conglomerate bedrock level; and (4) the modern period, in which the waves of expanding Western civilization broke upon East Asian shores and washed over the same ancient rocks. Chapter 5 deals with the present role and possible future of Confucianism in East Asia, and Chapter 6 with the new phase of interaction between East Asia and the West. There are, of course, other ways of looking at civilizations and other time frames one can set up. The foregoing, however, may best serve as the contribution I myself can make in a few chapters to the large and complicated business of understanding East Asia.

Knowledgeable readers will observe that, of the three major traditions, Taoism and Buddhism receive somewhat less attention here than Confucianism. The reason is that they had less of a role in defining those institutions and ideas most involved in the civil societies of East Asia as a whole and their modern transformation. In my view the strengths and weaknesses of a tradition tend to go together, as the Taoists especially were aware. The great strengths of Confucianism historically lay in the family, the school, and the state; its great problems likewise have lain in how these can coexist, and, if my historical analysis is correct, how all of these elements can relate to religion. Both Taoism and Buddhism had insight into these problems (as shown, for instance, by my references to *Chuang Tzu* and *Journey to the West* in dealing with the modern age), but they did not necessarily present any practical alternatives so far as civil society was concerned.

I should also explain my use of the term "dialogue." Here I use it to convey a sharing or exchange of ideas in the broadest sense, including even the effect of ideas and institutions upon each other, as people have reflected on choices to be made in crucial historical situations. In a more narrow sense the Confucians in particular favored conversational dialogue as a form of expression and an instrument of learning; so influential did this genre become that it found its way even into Ch'an Buddhism, though Ch'an (Zen) exchanges were thought of as essentially wordless communications.

Not everyone will be comfortable with such a loose use of the word, but in discussing East Asian civilizations in general terms, I have found no better way to describe the process of historical interaction among the great systems of thought and the major institutional configurations in East Asia. Perhaps "discourse" would do, but I reserve that term here for the explicit discursive learning that Neo-Confucians defended against the depreciation of it in Taoism and Zen. The kind of exchange I count as dialogue did not always take place through such discourse, that is, through direct debate or open acknowledgment of others' ideas. Nonetheless, through tacit dialogue significant advances were made at each major stage of East Asian history. Even the defense of traditional ideas and institutions, so often taken simply as a stubborn refusal to come to terms with others or adapt to change, has time and again incorporated new elements and cumulated in a richer, more complex development.

In the first stage, as I present it here, the dialogue is mainly among Confucianism, Mohism, Taoism, and Legalism; in the second stage it is among Buddhism, Confucianism, and the native traditions of other East Asian countries; in the third, between Neo-Confucianism and Buddhism; and in the fourth, mainly between Neo-Confucianism and Western civilization—each of these in a developing historical situation that called for some new response.

Finally I should express my regret that Vietnam, though part of East Asia and a participant in much of the dialogue discussed herein, remains a mute bystander in these pages. It is my hope that, by drawing attention to the shared traditions of East Asia, we will be reminded of the need for the deeper understanding of Vietnam that has so far eluded us, both in war and in peace.

These essays, the distillation of a lifetime's study of and reflection upon East Asian civilization, represent my own current thinking, and to the extent that anyone can take responsibility for his own work, I do so here. I would not, however, claim that they represent simply my own ideas. I have learned so much from others—from teachers, scholars, students over the years—that it does not seem worthwhile, when dealing with East Asia in such general terms, to try to separate out what is original with me and what has been borrowed from others. I can only acknowledge a very widespread indebtedness.

It probably would not have occurred to me to write so broadly and boldly about matters that do not lend themselves to succinct formulation had I not been challenged by the invitation from Roderick MacFarquhar and his committee to inaugurate the Reischauer Lectureship. Nevertheless the exercise, once undertaken, has proven to be a stimulating one for me, and I thank the John K. Fairbank Center for East Asian Research for prodding me into it. Even though I knew that I might expose more ignorance than expertise, I accepted the charge to discuss East Asian civilization as a whole in the spirit that anyone must have who still engages in general education today, that is, in the spirit of team teaching, hoping to learn more from one's colleagues than one is able to contribute oneself.

In the course of the discussions following my original presentation of the lectures, I have incurred debts to a number of colleagues and students for their questions and suggestions: Irene Bloom, Derk Bodde, Wing-tsit Chan, Ron-guey Chu, Margaret Chu, Elissa Cohen, Paul Cohen, Carol Gluck, Merle Goldman, Robert Hymes, Miwa Kai, Donald Keene, Gari Ledyard, John Schrecker, Arthur Tiedemann, John Tucker, and Paul Varley. As always, I have had wonderful support from my family, especially from Fanny Brett de Bary. In the preparation of the manuscript I have had the invaluable assistance of Emma Rockwell.

Contents

East Asian Civilizations

I The Classical Legacy

"IN THE BEGINNING WAS THE WORD," and in the morning of Chinese civilization the first words we know of were with gods, the ancestral deities to whom were addressed the questions recorded on Shang oracle bones. From these inscriptions we learn that the ruling classes of Shang China already held many of the values central to Chinese (and later East Asian) civilization: conceptions of reverence, filiality, kingly virtue, propriety in the performance of ritual, and so on. But these inscriptions, though already products of civilization in the sense that Shang society was literate and had most of the marks of a civil state, represent essentially a private communication between rulers and the spiritual beings claimed as the sources of their sovereignty or acknowledged as the disposers of their fate. In no sense are these messages addressed to us; they are neither statements to which we or other human beings might give assent nor questions to which we could have our own answers. Such consultations with the gods no doubt involved public functions, but not public utterance. The matters at issue had strictly to do with the proper business of rulers, ministers, diviners, and scribes, and the best we can do in such a case, even with all our modern skill at deciphering the code, is to listen in, not ourselves take part.

Portions of the *Book of Documents* and the *Book of Odes*

that are known to antedate Confucius are indeed addressed to a larger human audience, not just the gods. The limiting factor in this case is that they tend to be merely declaratory. Though proclaimed to "all under Heaven," the public they speak to is so vast and anonymous that its only function can be to listen. Whatever personal response there could have been to such declamations and celebrations would have to be inferred from a context established later by the Confucians. In the *Analects* Confucius spoke to the earlier traditions of the Chou dynasty, saying, "I follow Chou" (3:14). Much later, in 1982, when the modern philosopher Fung Yu-lan spoke at a Columbia convocation, he recalled a passage in the *Book of Odes,* "Chou is an ancient kingdom, but it has a new mission."[1] Fung identified himself as a surviving representative of Chinese civilization, subscribing to the same personal mission as Confucius and taking up the same dialogue.

Confucian dialogue proper, as the dialogue anyone could hope to enter into personally, starts with the opening lines of the *Analects* of Confucius:

> To study and in due season to practice what one has learned, is this not a pleasure?
> To have friends coming from afar, is that not a delight?
> To remain unembittered even though one is unrecognized, is that not to be a noble man [*chün-tzu*]?[2]

Here the interrogative voice and conversational tone mark this as a dialogue between Confucius and his companions, who will later record his discussions with them and thereby register their own concurrence in his rhetorical affirmations. More than this, however, Confucius invites one to take up a larger dialogue with past, present, and, in a sense, future. A passage in *Analects* 2:11 serves as all the gloss we need on these opening lines: "Appreciating the past and understanding the present, one can be a teacher of men."

Learning for Confucius meant the study of both past and present. Practice in turn meant applying the lessons of the past to one's own time. Above all, the most genuine satisfaction would come from learning to do something for oneself, that is, by actually doing it and not just learning how others had once done it. To delight in having friends come from afar implies a sharing of experience, a dialogue with others as much as a learning for oneself, a dialectical process between self and other that runs throughout life, and, as a theme, throughout the *Analects*. Capping this is the conception of the noble man, now no longer just a remnant nobleman who relies on birth and polite breeding to perpetuate an anachronistic social order, but a person whose largeness of soul triumphs over his ignominious lot and whose depth of practical wisdom enables him to be a teacher of men. For the would-be leader of men, it is not the hereditary privilege of the gentleman or nobleman that make him qualified, but only qualities of personal virtue that command respect, whether in the ruler or the teacher.

In his dialogue with the past Confucius drew upon virtues idealized earlier in the public roles of the sage-kings and their ministers, values known to have been held, whether or not they were actually lived up to, in the late Shang and early Chou. These values he transformed into an ethic of personal autonomy and responsibility, still within the spirit and ambience of the traditional ritual, but taking up much of the slack that social change had left in the customary understanding of roles and responsibilities. This was particularly significant for anyone, in or out of office, who saw himself as called to serve others. Mencius confirmed this transformation and universalization of the ethic when he spoke of the ranks of Heaven and the ranks of man, with individual qualities superseding in importance the definition of social ranks and privileges. Characteristically the new prescription claims the authority of highest antiquity:

> There is the nobility of Heaven and the nobility of man. Humaneness, rightness, being true to oneself and to one's word, unwearied joy in goodness—these are the nobility of Heaven. Duke, high minister, great officer—these are the ranks of human nobility. The ancients cultivated the nobility of Heaven and human ennoblement followed in its train. Today humans cultivate the nobility of Heaven only in the pursuit of ennobling rank, and having gained that, discard the cultivation of Heaven's nobility. This is the height of delusion. In the end they are certain to lose it all.   (*Mencius* 6A:16)

Confucius' insight not only anticipated Mencius' teaching, it looked to a future in which hereditary rank would dwindle almost to nothing in China, a day when, in the civil service or in the ranks of scholars, the moral and intellectual virtues alone would count as genuine worth. But Confucius, speaking to later generations of Chinese (and, as it turned out, East Asians) in all walks of life, also speaks to us and calls us to the same nobility.

Today this may sound a bit quaint and old-fashioned and make us a little uncomfortable, but it is, I think, what Confucius had in mind to do. When he said that the noble man is "unembittered even though unrecognized," he was not simply talking about gentlemanly accommodation or acquiescence in one's lot. As we know from other passages in the *Analects,* rather than accepting whatever comes as natural and inevitable, he called for a life of determined striving against adversity, taking part in an unceasing struggle to change the world:

One cannot flock with the birds or herd with the beasts. If not with other men of my own kind, with whom am I to associate? If the right Way already prevailed in the world, I would not be trying to change things. (*Analects* 16:6)

Wealth and rank are what every man desires, but if they cannot be obtained except at the expense of the Way, he does not accept them. Poverty and low station are what every man detests, but if it can only be done at the expense of the Way, avoiding them is not for him. The nobleman who departs from humanity—how can he be worthy of the name noble man? Never for a moment does the noble man forswear his humanity. Never is he so harried that he does not cleave to this, never so endangered that he does not cleave to this. (4:5)

For Confucius this was no amateur ideal, but a high calling, such that Arthur Waley, in his translation of the passage last cited, translates *Tao* as "the Way he professes." It is a profession in the original sense of practicing what one professes.

Conventionally speaking, the nobleman's business was to govern, but Confucius redefined this profession: "If you lead people by regimentation and regulate them by punishments, they will seek to evade the law and have no sense of shame. If you lead them by virtue and regulate them through rites, then, having a sense of shame, they will rectify themselves" (2:3). Some writers interpret the Confucian ethic as essentially based on an aristocratic code of honor, and they see the rites as strictly limited to the upper classes, but here (and elsewhere in the *Analects*) Confucius appeals not only to noblesse oblige but to the sense of self-respect found in all people and to the feeling of mutual trust that must underlie all true government.[3] Personal virtue and human rites are the basis of what Tu Wei-ming has aptly called the Confucian "fiduciary community."[4] Rites give defined form to human relations and suitable expression to the feelings of mutual respect that attach to all specific relationships. In a context of intimate familial and kinship relations, rather than impersonal legal ones, the rites serve somewhat the same function as human rights.

Thus it is understandable why Confucius most often describes this essential virtue as being truly human or humane (*jen*), and why this essential humanity, which he refuses to confine within formal definitions, may nevertheless be grasped through everyday experience. It is the practical product of self-reflection and an empathetic response to others (*shu*), at once personal and interpersonal, a process of dialogue between self and self, self and others, begun in the family and extended to the brotherhood of man. It is not just an accident of history that Confucius' teaching is best preserved in the *Analects;* its intimate dialogue expresses most truly how Confucius believed human virtue could be understood and cultivated in the company of others.

"Having friends come from afar" conveys Confucius' receptiveness to others and their experience of life, but his sense of mission also took him abroad to learn from others and share his own learning with them. In the same vein the opening lines of the *Mencius* picture a scene in which Mencius has "come from afar" to engage in dialogue with King Hui of the state of Liang. It is a dialogue between the ruler and one professing to be a teacher of rulers, who uses this opportunity to press further the implications of Confucius' view of humane government. Early in the dialogue, however, when Mencius gratuitously takes issue with the king's well-intentioned use of the word "profit" (*li*), we sense the unseen presence of another participant in the dialogue:

The king said: "You have not considered a thousand *li* too far to come, and must therefore have something of profit to offer my kingdom?" Mencius replied: "Why must you speak of profit? What I have to offer is humanity and rightness, nothing more. If a king says 'What will profit my kingdom?' the high officials will say 'what will profit our families?' and the lower officials and commoners will say, 'What will profit ourselves?' Superiors and inferiors will try to seize profit one from another, and the state will be endangered . . . Let your Majesty speak only of humanity and rightness. Why must you speak of profit?" (1A:1)

In fact King Hui speaks of profit not only because most princes think of it as something beneficial, but also because he is made to stand in for Mencius' antagonist Mo Tzu, just off stage, and to raise the issue of what really is of benefit to the people. In other words King Hui is being set up as the unwitting foil for Mo Tzu's utilitarianism, which is now part of the larger dialogue of early Chinese thought. Mo Tzu, indeed, represents a challenge Mencius cannot avoid, intellectually speaking, even if he prefers as always to stand on his own dignity and not acknowledge Mo Tzu's presence. The dialogue so encountered is hardly a fair debate or genuine exchange with Mo Tzu, but, one-sided though the presentation may be, Mencius shows that he has been listening to the Mohist critique of Confucianism and will lay out a whole range of counterarguments in the rest of the book.

The appeal of Mo Tzu's position is twofold: its sentiments are broad and humanitarian, and its objectives are simple and utilitarian: food, clothing, and shelter for the people. Mencius proceeds to expose the shallowness of the broad sentiments (appearing here in the guise of the king's professed concern for his people) in two ways: first, by showing how deep an understanding of and commitment to moral principles is needed if anything practical is to come of the king's good intentions, and second, by showing how practicality or utility is to be understood if in the long run it is to serve truly human ends. "There are those with humane intentions and a reputation for humanitarianism, and yet the people enjoy no benefit from them, nor do they leave any model (*fa*) for later generations to follow, all because they have failed to enact the ways of the ancient kings. Therefore it is said, 'In government it is not enough simply to pursue good intentions' while [on the other hand] the pursuit of laws and systems (*fa*) alone will not be enough for their effective implementation" (4A:1).

In context Mencius is saying that commitments to both virtue and specific, time-tested models or laws are needed for the actual achievement of humane government. In the dialogue with King Hui of Liang, Mencius goes on to discuss in detail the different systems enacted by the ancient kings. We have reason to doubt that any of these systems existed in exactly the form Mencius describes, but they serve as excellent paradigms for didactic purposes. Mencius invokes the ideal of the sage-kings, as Confucius had done, in order to validate and illustrate a whole infrastructure of political economy and social organization that will ensure dispersion of power and wealth throughout the kingdom, so that humane government can be administered in personalized form, as in a kinship system, rather than through impersonal, bureaucratic procedures. It is a decentralized enfeoffment system, but in contrast to Western or Japanese "feudalism," it has a clear center. One cannot call it pluralistic or polycentric, because Mencius, like most thinkers of his day, assumes that the essential problem is how to reconstitute human society around a true center. Nevertheless he is equally concerned about the overconcentration of power, the need for outspoken ministers to check its abuse at court, and the importance of fixing both authority and responsibility (with the material means to carry them out) on successive levels and in measured degrees throughout a graded structure of delegated power. Self-respect and self-reliance depend on material self-sufficiency, and no one is more pointed than Mencius on the need for ministers to maintain their own self-respect and independence of the ruler, lest they become "kept" as mere hirelings, no better than concubines or playthings of their master.

In laying this out, with apt and memorable illustrations of basic principles (the well-field system, the system of enfeoffment with its exactly proportioned assignments of land, the tax system, and so on), Mencius deals concretely with many problems of political and economic organization that Mo Tzu had sped past in his intensely earnest but headlong rush to mobilize all resources in line with a simple totalitarian vision. Much the same is true of the contrast between Mo Tzu's simplistic assumptions regarding human behavior and Mencius' more probing analysis of human nature—what motivates and conditions human behavior, the relation of body and mind, intellect and affections, and so on. These matters were of great consequence to Mencius' view of humane government, which could not serve its purpose without taking into account the full dimensions and complexity of man's humanity.

Discussion of Mencius and human nature almost invariably invites comparison to the other great Confucian thinker of that age, Hsun Tzu, and to the conception of human nature as evil that is found in one chapter of the book bearing his name. Actually, viewed in terms of what is essential to the development of the Confucian canon in the formative stage, there is far more agreement between Mencius and Hsun Tzu on basic issues than there is disagreement. Hence it is not warranted to take a possible theoretical difference between them over whether human nature is good or evil and escalate it into a thoroughgoing opposition on all crucial points. Indeed, to construe this as constituting the great debate within classical Confucianism may obscure an even more significant

controversy between Hsun Tzu and the Taoists and Legalists.
Here again the matter is not aired in open debate, nor is there
a fair exchange of opposing views, but from the opening lines
of the *Hsun Tzu*'s first chapter, "An Encouragement to
Learning," we become aware of how powerfully Hsun Tzu is
challenged by the Taoist critique of Confucian learning and
how urgent is the need he feels, in the-face of a more radical
questioning of civilization and scholarship than had appeared
before, to offer a reasoned defense of human culture. Against
the charge that intellectual effort is unnatural and that all
value distinctions are artificial, Hsun Tzu argues the benefits
of civilization for the enhancement of human life and insists
that it is impossible to escape making moral choices and
intellectual distinctions. Intuition, improvisation, and moral
detachment are no substitutes for systematic study, refined
judgment, and informed decision making when one faces critical junctures in life: "If there is no dark and dogged will,
there will be no shining accomplishment; if there is no dull
and determined effort, there will be no brilliant achievement.
He who tries to travel two roads at once will arrive nowhere;
he who serves two masters will please neither."[5]

Hsun Tzu goes on to present his own conception of an
educational program, which includes what is probably the
first definition of a classical Confucian curriculum, keyed to
the life process of human growth and maturation.

> If you truly pile up effort over a long period of time, you
> will enter into the highest realm. Learning continues un-
> til death and only then does it cease. Therefore we may
> speak of an end to the program of learning, but the
> objective of learning must never for an instant be given
> up. To pursue it is to be a man, to give it up is to become
> a beast. The *Book of Documents* is the record of govern-
> ment affairs, the *Odes* the repository of correct sounds,
> and the *Rites* the great basis of law and the foundation

of precedents. Therefore learning reaches its completion with the rites, for they may be said to represent the highest point of the Way and its power. The reverence and order of the rites, the fitness and harmony of music, the breadth of the *Odes* and *Documents,* the subtlety of the *Spring and Autumn Annals*—these encompass all that is between heaven and earth.[6]

Although Hsun Tzu's view of heaven, earth, and man shows some influence of Taoist naturalism, his conception of true learning excludes much that he saw as supernatural and occult but that today we might see as protoscientific. Stubbornly rationalistic and somewhat narrowly humanistic, he nevertheless has a strong feeling for a deep, integral learning: "The learning of the gentleman enters his ear, clings to his mind, spreads through his four limbs, and manifests itself in his actions. His smallest word, his slightest movement can serve as a model. The learning of the petty man enters his ear and comes out his mouth. With only four inches between ear and mouth, how can he have possession of it long enough to ennoble a seven-foot body?"[7]

According to Hsun Tzu, the petty man fails to make use of others' erudition or to associate with men who love learning: "If you are first of all unable to love such men and secondly are incapable of honoring rites, then you will only be learning a mass of jumbled facts, blindly following the *Odes* and *Documents* and nothing more. In such a case you may study to the end of your days and you will never be anything but a vulgar pedant."[8] But if one stays the course of true learning, Hsun Tzu says: "One's mind will feel keener delight in it than in the possession of empire. When one has reached this stage, one cannot be subverted by power or the love of profit; one cannot be swayed by the masses; one cannot be moved by the world. One follows this one thing in life; one follows it in death. This is what is called constancy of virtue. One who has such constancy of virtue can order himself, and, having ordered himself, can then respond to others. Ordering oneself and responding to others—this is to achieve fulfillment as a human being."[9]

Even in this abridged and truncated form one can, I think, appreciate something of Hsun Tzu's eloquence in articulating the ideal of the noble man as scholar—a role which was to prove of cardinal importance for the later development of Confucianism. Here we glimpse at once the impressive stature and resplendent glory of the Confucian ideal of learning, as well as perhaps some of the limitations in its prospective historical role.

Before proceeding to the later development, however, we should take note of what Hsun Tzu has to say about rites, which he has acclaimed as the very summit and completion of learning—indeed, as the "highest point of the Way and its power." He is as eloquent about this matter as he is about the glories of Confucian scholarship, and the two together were to become foundation stones of the classical Confucian tradition. Unfortunately Hsun Tzu has often been misread on the subject of rites because of the too facile assumption that his low estimate of human nature logically demands the imposition of rigid social constraints. Actually Hsun Tzu's key chapter on rites has little of this; it is based rather on the idea that human desires are natural and must be satisfied:

Whence do the rites arise? From the fact that men are born with desires, and when desires are not satisfied, men are bound to pursue them. When that pursuit is carried on without limit or measure, there is bound to be contention. With contention comes disorder and with disorder exhaustion. The ancient kings hated such disorder and set the necessary limits by codifying rites and rightness, so that desires would be nourished and their pursuit gratified. In this way they saw to it that desires would not be exhausted by things nor things exhausted by desires. Thus the two should sustain each other and thrive together. This is whence the rites arise.[10]

From this assertion that rites are the means of satisfying and sustaining human desires, Hsun Tzu goes on to argue the need for making value distinctions and establishing social disciplines appropriate to the cultivation and refinement of the desires themselves. The sense appetites thus represent a good, a power to be both nourished and conserved by rites. Here is a premise in strong contrast to a prevalent assumption in Indian religion, and especially in early Buddhism, that desires are a source of suffering and delusion from which one must be liberated. Instead of extinguishing desires or emancipating oneself from them, Hsun Tzu's concept of human freedom is to bring about such an ordering of desires and the means of their satisfaction that the two are commensurate with one another, and fulfillment can be achieved in the present, earthly condition, that is, within the form of things. This ideal may not be unique to the Chinese, but it is certainly a Utopian vision in keeping with the Chinese appetite for life and, in the later political life of China, with a recurring faith that Heaven, in the sense of a rational moral order, can be embodied in the social order—in other words, that man can achieve Heaven-on-Earth.

It is generally accepted that the early development of the Confucian school through the Han dynasty was marked more by the social and scholarly vision of Hsun Tzu than by Mencius' more voluntaristic philosophy. Actually, in respect to most political and social institutions, there is little difference in their views, but in respect to the codification of rites, the definition of the classical canon, and the promotion of systematic scholarship, Hsun Tzu better articulates the rationale for Confucian learning that triumphed in the Han.

Often that triumph has been explained in terms of the need

of the Han dynasty, as an empire founded by a commoner with no claim to inheritance from an earlier feudal house, for an ideology that would legitimize its power, a ritual that would dignify its court, and a scholarly class that could staff the offices of its centralized bureaucratic administration. One cannot discount these as factors in the increasing collaboration of Han rulers and Confucian scholars. The late A. L. Basham, a leading Indologist, saw this collaboration as providing Chinese dynasties with a stability and a continuity, based on secular learning and a bureaucratic ethos, that Indian dynasties lacked.[11]

However this may be, no less significant is that Confucian learning survived on its own through scholarly lineages, and in Chinese homes as a family ethic, long before it gained official recognition or dynastic sponsorship. Even its critics, whether Mohist, Taoist, or Legalist, testify to the central role and wide influence of Confucian teachings in Chinese life, despite the Chinese rulers' continuing indifference to them, not to mention the actual contempt of some and even suppression by others. In the face of such resistance, Confucianism's survival into Han times cannot be explained by the sporadic use of Confucian rituals as dynastic window dressing or the occasional cooptation of individual scholars alone; instead it must indicate that Confucianism became an established teaching independently of the imperial state.

On the other hand, it would be equally unreal to picture Confucianism as standing solely on its own, aloof from government, or to consider only those scholars and teachers who refrained from participation in government as true to the teaching of Confucius and Mencius (who themselves saw little official service). One cannot take as formative of a tradition only its fountainheads, with the freshness and simplicity of their original inspiration, and fail to reckon with those adherents who plunged into the muddy waters of Chinese imperial politics. Without the latter it is even less likely that the tradition would have survived in its historic form.

In the early records one finds a strong consciousness that the Han dynasty is heir to the Ch'in, not to the Chou. It has continued, largely unchanged, the Ch'in structure of Legalist-type systems. As a centralized autocratic and bureaucratic state the Han stands at a far remove, in its concentration of power and impersonal administration, from the Confucian ideal of decentralized, personalized, and paternalistic rule or the Mencian conception of the delegation and dispersal of power. Yet at least by the reign of the Emperor Wu (140–87 B.C.) the new imperial system has become well established, and the model institutions of the early Chou are seen as anachronistic—far removed in the past and unlikely to be resurrected. In short, the Confucians are faced with a historic change that seems irreversible. As a historic dilemma it is somewhat comparable to the situation of the Chinese today who may not have supported Mao's revolution but who have to decide, even in the face of the disasters brought on by the Gang of Five, whether to resort to more violence, drop out altogether, or cooperate with the new system, hoping to modify and moderate it.

When is one accepting unyielding realities, and when is one making unacceptable compromises with an inhumane system? The answer of Han Confucians, by and large, was that it depended less on the system than on the man—on a man's understanding of changing times, on how enduring principles can be adapted to a changed situation, and on how systems can be changed to accord better with humane principles. The leading Confucian scholar in the time of the great Emperor Wu, Tung Chung-shu (179–104 B.C.), accepted official appointment as a professor of the classics and was a key figure in the establishment of the Confucian classics as the basis of public instruction, but he was also widely respected as a person of great integrity and as an outspoken advocate of political and economic reforms. Tung was an authority on the classic *Spring and Autumn Annals,* a chronicle purportedly concerned with how Confucian principles were interpreted and applied to actual human affairs. In Tung's critical dialogue with Legalism and its embodiment in Han institutions, he made a significant concession to the need for laws and systems. A ruler should rely primarily on moral example and education (*chiao-hua*), appealing to man's better nature and his capability for self-transformation. But a necessary complement to the power of positive (*yang*) thinking was the negative (*yin*) sanction represented by laws and by the application of organized power and coercive force to those who showed themselves unresponsive to moral suasion.

In balancing and blending these two approaches, the key was to choose or train the right man to exercise the necessary judgment in office. But as Tung faced the problem, even more crucial was the education of the "one man," the dynastic ruler, who represented a simple given in that situation and was not, for Tung, a matter of choice as to whom else he might support or advise. The Confucian could not be responsive to the needs of the times without undertaking to educate and advise the man in power, and this could not be done without running the risk of the Confucian scholar's conferring some legitimacy on a ruler whose actions he could, at best, only influence, not control.

Tung's description of this ambivalent situation is as follows:

> The ruler is the basis of the state. In administering the state, nothing is more effective for educating the people than reverence for the basis. If the basis is revered then the ruler may transform the people as though by supernatural power, but if the basis is not revered the ruler will have nothing by which to lead his people. Then, though he employ harsh penalties and severe punishments, the people will not follow him. This is to drive the state to ruin, and there is no greater disaster.
>
> What do we mean by the basis? Heaven, earth, and

man are the basis of all creatures. Heaven gives them birth, earth nourishes them, and man brings them to completion. Heaven provides them at birth with a sense of filial and brotherly love, earth nourishes them with clothing and food, and man completes them with rites and music. The three act together as hands and feet join to complete the body and none can be dispensed with ... If all three are lacking, then the people will become like deer, each person following his own desires, each family possessing its own ways.

Fathers cannot employ their sons nor rulers their ministers, and though there be walls and battlements they will be called an "empty city." Then will the ruler lie down with a clod of earth for a pillow. No one menacing him, he will endanger himself; no one destroying him, he will destroy himself.[12]

Here we see that underlying the collaboration of Confucian ministers with Chinese rulers, exposed as this situation was to the danger of cooptation, lay the hope of persuading rulers that the great power they held (nothing the Confucians had given them) should be matched by a commensurate sense of responsibility to Heaven for the welfare of its people (about which Confucians had much to say).

Tung's views concerning the ordering of human society were similar to Hsun Tzu's in that he placed primary reliance on rites and aimed at keeping a balanced proportion between people's needs and desires and the material means of satisfying them. The concentration of wealth upset this balance. A concrete example is found in what Tung had to say about the pressing land problem in his day. Here again we note the compromise between the ideal and the practical. After citing the ancient ideal of land holding and minimal taxation, Tung describes the catastrophic changes made by the Ch'in dynasty:

Unbalanced power

It used the methods of Shang Yang [Legalism], altered the imperial institutions, did away with the well-field system, and allowed the people to buy and sell land. The rich bought up great connecting tracts of ground, and the poor were left without enough land to stick the point of an awl into . . . In addition labor services were increased until they were thirty times those of ancient days, while taxes on fields and population and profits from salt and iron increased to twenty times those of old. Those who worked the land of the rich had to give half their crops in rent. Therefore the poor were forced to wear clothing fit only for cattle and horses and eat the food of dogs and swine. On top of this, harsh and greedy officials punished and executed them indiscriminately until the people, grieved and deprived of their livelihood, fled to the hills or turned to a life of banditry. Condemned men half filled the roads and tens of thousands were imprisoned each year.

Since the Han began it has followed the ways of the Ch'in without change. Although it would be difficult to restore at once the ancient well-field system, it is proper that present usage be brought somewhat closer to the old ways. Ownership of land should be limited so that those who do not have enough may be relieved and the road to unlimited encroachment blocked.[13]

Tung's relatively moderate solution was not implemented, and the land problem continued to worsen through the Former Han dynasty, until, at the turn of the millennium another Confucian scholar-statesman, Wang Mang (33 B.C.–A.D. 23), undertook more drastic reforms in the name of the Confucian welfare state. Politically speaking, he too failed, but the combination of strong measures he sought to carry out—nationalization and redistribution of land in the name of the ancient well-field system and vigorous reenactment of government monopolies and marketing controls—involved a powerful intrusion of the state into the economy and the adoption of Legalist-type institutions with a seeming Confucian justification.

Such an amalgam of Confucian theory and Legalist practice became almost standard in the later Chinese political tradition, oscillating between the pole of Tung Chung-shu's view of moderate reformism, with minimal state involvement in the economy, and the opposite pole of Wang Mang's more radical interventions through strong state initiatives and controls. It is significant, however, that Legalist policies and systems became so much a part of the Confucian political repertoire (as was seen again in the policies of the great Sung reformer Wang An-shih) that a description of them was included, almost two millennia later, in a Ph.D. dissertation for Columbia entitled "The Economic Principles of Confucius and His School." There they were waiting to be discovered by Henry Wallace, who faced similar economic dilemmas in the days of Roosevelt's New Deal. From his reading in this book, Wallace drew the idea of the ever-normal granary, incorporated in the Agricultural Adjustment Act of 1938.[14] "Ever-normal granary" is a literal translation from the Chinese model he adopted. It was a matter of even less consequence to Wallace than to Chinese practitioners of Confucian statecraft that the system had a Legalist provenance. More important was that it served the professed humane purposes of a reformist welfare state seeking to achieve economic balance and price stability.

In conclusion I would characterize the Chinese tradition as it emerged from its formative stage as in the main a synthesis of classical Confucianism, deeply rooted in the school and family, with the institutions of the Han state, which was impressive in its control of a populous and productive agrarian economy but was already showing the strains of managing so vast an enterprise. The record, of course, exhibited both successes and failures. The combined cultural legacy of this civilization to later generations was a rich literature including the Confucian canon, with its ethical teachings, political lore, history, poetry, and ritual texts; important alternative teachings in the texts of Taoism, Legalism, Mohism, and so on; and major records of the Chinese dynastic experience. Among its central values I have highlighted the learning and moral responsibility of the noble man, the Confucian paradigm for the individual or person, along with the ritual order in the family or kinship system as the structure and process best embodying the ideal of the Confucian fiduciary community. But embedded in the Han histories, Han law, and Han institutions were important adaptations of these traditional values to the realities of Chinese life in the first imperial age.

In the next stage we shall see what a profound impression this legacy made on other peoples when it was carried to less advanced countries of East Asia. It was carried abroad, however, not by Confucian scholars, nor by Legalist experts, nor by Han armies. The forces that had come together to construct the great Han civilization proved unable to make the center hold, much less to defend the borders. Han power and Confucian teaching had failed to fulfill Hsun Tzu's aspiration of creating Heaven-on-Earth, and with the dynasty in shambles at the end of the second century, the Confucian scholar had to fall back on the Book of Changes, biding his time and looking for some oracular sign that a new day would break from the encircling gloom. It was left to foreign conquest and a foreign religion to set the stage for the next great epoch in East Asian civilization.

2 | The Buddhist Age

FROM A PURELY CHINESE historical perspective it is significant that Buddhism made deep inroads into China at a time of political and military disarray, when traditional institutions were least able to mount their cultural defenses. Some observers would see the Chinese as particularly susceptible at that time to a foreign, otherworldly faith because it offered an anodyne for people's suffering in a disordered age. A view plausible enough, one might say, in the devastated north, where under foreign conquest the dislocation of life and disruption of native tradition was extreme. In central and south China, however, where the Chinese were extending their frontiers and the economy was expanding, the picture is not one of widespread hardship and deprivation. On the contrary, the life of the elite that furnished the leaders of the so-called gentry Buddhism often appears affluent and self-indulgent. In the literature of the period there is a certain joie de vivre and even libertinism, on the other side of which lies a jaded and decadent hedonism. Meanwhile the sophisticated Neo-Taoist philosophy of nothingness and normlessness, prevalent in the third century, betrays a widespread ennui and anomie among an intelligentsia that had once felt called to public service but was now skeptical of the old values and civic virtues. The educated class had seen the center of their world collapse, and with this their world-ordering mission—the dream of achieving Heaven-on-Earth—had fallen to the ground. A profound spiritual malaise, more deep-seated than physical hunger, seems to have set in.

It is precisely to this condition of life, however, that Buddhism addresses itself. In the legends of the Buddha's life, after he has left the pleasures of the palace and witnessed the sufferings of humankind, his response to this shocking experience is revealing. He did not rush to help the afflicted nor did he return to his palace, hoping to redirect the use of power toward the amelioration of social evils or the relief of human distress. Rather he set out on a long and determined religious quest, seeking a more fundamental answer to the problem than mere external remedies or temporary palliatives could provide.

Addressing the human predicament in this way, the Buddha arrived at his own diagnosis, that life inherently involves suffering and that suffering arises from desire or selfish craving, assertions that seem in stark contrast to earlier Chinese assumptions, especially to the Chinese relish for life. Along with this pessimistic analysis, however, he offered a prognosis and prescription that were highly optimistic. Selfish craving, he said, could be extinguished, and he even gave a specific method for accomplishing this: the Noble Eightfold Path of self-disciplined thought and conduct leading to right concentration of mind, in which meditative state one would attain enlightenment and experience the peace of Nirvana.

By the time Buddhism reached China this basic doctrine and method of practice had become greatly elaborated but also in some ways modified. One of the most significant changes in the Mahayana form of Buddhism, as it came to China, was that the conception of Buddhahood largely superseded Nirvana as the goal of religious attainment. This was especially dramatized in the *Lotus Sūtra*, destined to become the most popular religious scripture throughout East Asia. Dismissing the earlier so-called Hinayana teaching as essentially negative and limited, the *Lotus* dwelt, not on an indefinable and colorless Nirvana, but on the resplendent personal attributes of the Buddha and the compassionate help of the bodhisattvas. All beings were now assured that they possessed the seeds of Buddhahood and that with the aid of the bodhisattvas they could bring these seeds to fruition—again, a prospect far more attractive to most people than the difficult ascent to Nirvana via the Eightfold Path, a path few were able to pursue to its destination.

The language of the *Lotus,* with its glorification of the Buddhas, bodhisattvas, and other heavenly beings, was appealing enough in itself, but Buddhist painting and sculpture further stirred people's religious imaginations. It is striking that at this time, in contrast to earlier Chinese art, which drew mainly on animal forms and human social scenes for its subject matter, a Buddhist art appeared that glorified the individual human figure and gave vivid expression to moral and spiritual qualities—detachment, serenity of mind, calm resolution, courage, lofty aspiration, wisdom, compassion—that had not been given artistic expression before. To some extent this change may reflect an earlier Buddhist encounter with Hellenistic art in northwest India, before Buddhism made its transcontinental journey to the East. In any case it is significant that this seemingly transcendental religion, in which the religious life was often described as "leaving the world" or "leaving the home," should have served as a vehicle for such a humanizing of Chinese, and in fact East Asian, art. Accustomed as we are to thinking of Confucianism and the Chinese tradition as humanistic and of Indian religions as "otherworldly," it is a challenge to our preconceptions to realize that Buddhism had this kind of humanizing influence on the Chinese. That it could have performed such a function indicates how the experience of transcendence can be a profoundly human and culturally energizing one, even when the religion in question seems to stand in radical opposition to other human values.

In this case two of the most fundamental and paradigmatic activities of early Buddhism—meditation and preaching—were faithfully represented in typical poses of the Buddha figure. Meditation was as intrinsic to the religion as enlightenment; preaching was optional inasmuch as enlightenment, once attained, freed one from any obligation or compulsion to proselytize. Nevertheless, scriptures early and late, Hinayana and Mahayana, portray the Buddha as preaching and instructing his followers to preach. It is sometimes said that Indian religions are not missionary religions, and this is certainly true of Confucianism as well. But it is fair to say that in contrast to the concern of Hinduism with caste and class, and of Confucianism with kinship and community, Buddhism was from its beginning a homeless wisdom, a mendicant and missionary religion.

This fact is of the greatest importance for understanding the historic role of Buddhism in East Asia. As a meditative religion it could be called inward-looking, but it looked inward at no center, at no substantial self or definable nature, and as a preaching or missionary religion it looked outward on a world with no fixed center of authority. In doctrinal terms this is true of any school of Buddhism premised on the insubstantiality of the self or the untenability of any fixed view of truth—a position identified with the teaching of Emptiness. In religious terms Emptiness was expressed, as in the *Lotus* and *Vimalakirti* sūtras especially, by the principle of adaptive means: Emptiness seen as infinitely adaptable to the condition or consciousness of the believer. Finally, in artistic terms this truth could be represented by the innumerable mudras, or hand signs, of the Buddha or by the thousand arms of the compassionate bodhisattva Avalokitesvara. In most Chinese and Japanese representations of the bodhisattva as Kuan-yin or Kwannon, these many arms are empty-handed save one: the hand that carries the lamp of enlightenment.

Such being the case, Buddhism was free, on reaching East Asia, to shed any of the Indian garments in which it had been clothed, while its hands were free to pick up new cultural baggage and carry it forward. In the process Buddhism helped bring to Korea and Japan much of the classical legacy of China in the form of philosophy, literature, and the arts, as well as Han ideas and institutions.

In the early encounters of Buddhism with Chinese tradition, as for instance in the dialogue identified with Mou Tzu, we find numerous difficulties in the translation and adaptation of Buddhist concepts.[1] Not surprisingly, many of these center on differing views of self, soul, body, the afterlife, and so on, few of which difficulties would ever be definitively resolved on the conceptual plane. On the practical level, however, Buddhism sooner or later adapted itself to most of the Chinese family system and political institutions. It was able to do this because, except for the religious life's specific demand that one "leave the world" (and even this was applicable only in a limited sense to lay Buddhism), and except for its urging the ruler to promote and protect the religion as a source of spiritual benefits, Buddhism had little to say specifically about the organization and conduct of family life or the state. Empty-handed in these respects, it remained free to adapt to native tastes.[2]

This process of adaptation and of Buddhism's further extension into Korea and Japan was well begun before China was reunified under the Sui and T'ang dynasties. Hence when Buddhism appeared elsewhere in East Asia it was not seen primarily as an expansion of Chinese power or influence but rather as an extension of Buddhism's progress across Asia and penetration to the outer rim of East Asia—this at a time of political fragmentation and cultural disorientation on the mainland and of rapid historical change in Korea and Japan. That Buddhism could contribute to a new process of state building in seventh- and eighth-century Korea and Japan was again, as I see it, a function of its spiritual dynamism and adaptability to new situations. It could serve as a solvent of old loyalties and excipient of new ones.

This was neither the first nor the last time that religion would serve as a carrier of civilization in forms not intrinsic to its own spiritual message but rather responsive to new historical situations. In modern times Christian missionaries performed much the same cultural function in East Asia. The full story of their contribution to civilization remains to be told, but if one thinks of the missionary A. K. Reischauer as representative of a band of pioneers in the development of East-West understanding, one may hope that their contribution will attract more serious study, at the same time that we are coming to recognize how Buddhist missionaries and pilgrims made a similar contribution centuries before.

In the earlier case we can see how the universalistic doctrines of Buddhism could function as a solvent of the particularistic loyalties that had characterized the clan-dominated society of early Japan, while Buddhism itself first took on some of the coloration of clan religion and then, as it participated in the process of state-building, became a kind of "state religion," promoted from the beginning with imperial patronage and protection. Possessing, as I said earlier, no determinate center of authority of its own, Buddhism readily lent itself to acceptance of imperial authority. The real problem would be whether the imperial authority—the political center itself—could be maintained. One cannot equate this historical situation with T'ang dynasty China. There the state was a deeply entrenched force, whereas at the dawning of civilized life (that is, literate, citified society) in Japan, nothing about the outcome was inevitable except perhaps that Japan's own indigenous traditions—polycentric, particularistic, and strongly hierarchical—would be the most likely determinants of the result.

At this point we may consider at closer hand a most remarkable statement of the matter in what has become known as the "Seventeen Article Constitution" of Prince Shōtoku, attributed to the Japanese statesman who led in the adoption of both Buddhism and the Chinese political system in the early seventh century. Questions have long been asked about the actual authorship and dating of this document, but even if everything in the Seventeen Articles is not by Shōtoku's own hand, few scholars have doubted that they are generally representative of his thinking.[3] Since the text appears in the *Nihon shoki* (A.D. 720), it must in any case reflect views current in the early state-building period and, as recorded in that early chronicle, it became canonical as one of the founding myths of Japan. More than that, however, there are signs of a singular intelligence at work in its composition.[4]

Although the term *kempō*, applied in the original text to the Seventeen Articles, has been used since the late nineteenth century for "constitution" in the modern Western sense, its original meaning was more like "exemplary law" or "basic model." The term had few of the legalistic connotations attaching to modern constitutions, not being intended as the ultimate recourse for a judicial system but rather as a set of basic moral precepts and political guidelines for the conduct of government. In this respect the Seventeen Articles resemble more the very general provisions of the U.S. Bill of Rights, of which it has been said that they would be meaningless if it were not for the rest of the Constitution. "What makes it work, what assures that these are not just hollow promises, is the structure of government that the original Constitution established, the checks and balances of government."[5] In the Seventeen Articles there is scant evidence of such a structure, of checks and balances, or of a strict separation of powers. It was only with the later adoption of T'ang-type law codes that

such structure and definition developed, at least to the extent
of getting something on the books.

In the Seventeen Articles, true to the Chinese concept,
there is a clear assertion of central authority, but this is accompanied by a most extraordinary qualification of it, with
other strands of both Chinese and non-Chinese thought wo-
ven into its loose fabric. Evidence of this appears in the first
article: "Harmony is to be valued and contentiousness
avoided. All men are inclined to partisanship and few are
truly discerning . . . But when those above are harmonious
and those below conciliatory, and when there is concord in
the discussion of all matters, the disposition of affairs comes
about naturally. Then what is there that cannot be accomplished?"[6] The language used here is found in Confucian
texts like the *Analects* and the *Record of Rites,* and the general spirit too is Confucian, but the sentiments are universal
and no less acceptable to Buddhism or, one might assume in
the absence of earlier records, to native Japanese tradition.
Synthesis and consensus are the primary values here, not the
assertion of one tradition over another.

The second article affirms the basic importance of Buddhism's spiritual contribution to the social order: "Sincerely
reverence the Three Treasures. The Buddha, the Law, and the
Religious orders are the final refuge of all beings and the
supreme objects of reverence in all countries. It is a law hon-
ored by all, no matter what the age or who the person. Few
men are utterly bad; with instruction they can follow it. But if
they do not betake themselves to the Three Treasures, how
can their crookedness be made straight?"[7] This is the only
explicit reference to Buddhism in the Seventeen Articles and
might be seen as a mere token. Yet Buddhism was not actually an established church, to which convention might dic-
tate a perfunctory show of respect. On the contrary it appears here (in Shōtoku's eyes) as a new dispensation, to be
welcomed by the Japanese as it has come to be accepted

everywhere else, by all nations and peoples, as a universal teaching. The fact that Shōtoku does not draw any specifically political conclusions from Buddhism, however, is significant. There are, in fact, none to be drawn. Rather Buddhism functions at a deeper level of consciousness, where one must reach underlying human motivations if one is to cope with the deeper disorders of the spirit ("men's crookedness"), with which the ruler would ultimately have to reckon.

The next four articles deal with typically Han Confucian concerns: the upholding of the structure of political authority as represented by the hierarchy of Heaven, Earth, and Man; rites as the essential instruments of social order; the lesser role of laws; and the proper handling of litigation, punishments, and rewards. These already involve a synthesis of Confucian and Legalist approaches, and one can almost hear the voice of the Han scholar, Tung Chung-shu himself, speaking. But the Seventh Article raises in a new form the old issue of laws and impersonal systems, versus men and personal character, as the mainstay of government:

Let every man have his own charge, and let not the spheres of duty be confused. When wise and worthy men are entrusted with office, the sound of praise arises. If unprincipled men hold office, disasters and tumults multiply. In this world, few are born with knowledge; wisdom is the product of earnest meditation. In all things, whether great or small, find the right man, and they will surely be well managed; on all occasions, be they urgent or the reverse, meet but with a wise and worthy man, and they will of themselves be amenable. In this way the State will be lasting and the Temples of the Earth and of Grain will be free from danger. Therefore did the wise sovereigns of antiquity seek the man to fill the office, and not the office for the sake of the man.[8]

If one compares this with the quotation in Chapter 1 from Tung Chung-shu concerning the crucial role of the ruler, one notices that Shōtoku's discussion is directed at ministers and officials, discreetly avoiding any reference to the emperor, upon whose person Tung in Han China had directly placed the primary responsibility. In the Tenth Article, after underscoring the importance of conscientiousness and mutual trust in the conduct of affairs (the essential "fiduciary" character of government), Shōtoku returns to the subject of wisdom and virtue in those who govern. At this juncture he makes some surprising observations:

> Let us not be resentful when others differ from us. For all men have their hearts and each heart has its own leanings. Their right is our wrong, and our right is their wrong. We are not unquestionably sages, nor are they unquestionably fools. Both of us are simply ordinary men. How can any one lay down a rule by which to distinguish right from wrong? For we are all, one with another, wise and foolish, like a ring which has no end.
>
> Therefore, although others give way to anger, let us on the contrary dread our own faults, and though we alone may be in the right, let us follow the multitude and act like them.[9]

Here again direct reference to the emperor is avoided, and the discussion is kept at the level of ordinary men, but on that level is exposed, with startling candor and realism, the problem of human fallibility. Instead of invoking the authority of Heaven and the moral certainties it vouchsafes, Shōtoku disavows any pretensions to sagely authority and puts himself on the level of other men. In Buddhist terms the only significant distinction is between the enlightened and the unenlightened; both rulers and ruled alike fall into the latter category as ordinary men.[10] Furthermore, implied here is a

Buddhist skepticism in regard to truth, based on the Emptiness view. This lends itself to, and is in turn reinforced by, a Japanese disinclination to involve the sacred (that is, the throne) in the profane. In other words, there is a disposition to maintain a certain distance between religion and morality, between the numinous realm and the conduct of human affairs. (This preference was confirmed later in the Japanese choice of the word *tennō* for the emperor, a Chinese term identified with the god of the northern quarter of the city, where the imperial palace stood, rather than one associated with a moral mandate from Heaven, which might expose to question the claim of the ruling house to unbroken hereditary succession.)[11]

Shōtoku keeps referring to this issue. In the Fourteenth Article it comes up again, as an unavoidable confrontation between the Confucian view of sagely rule and a more skeptical view of human nature: "The evils of envy know no limit. If others excel us in intelligence, it gives us no pleasure; if they surpass us in ability, we are envious. Therefore it is only after the lapse of five hundred years that we meet a wise man, and even in a thousand we can hardly welcome one sage. But if we do not find sages and worthies, wherewithal shall the country be governed?"[12] Here Shōtoku frankly confronts the contradiction between the Confucian faith in human intelligence and virtue and, influenced by a measure of Buddhist skepticism, a realistic assessment of these qualities. He has, however, a way to cope with this seeming dilemma. As he says in Article Fifteen, individuals should subordinate their selfish interests and private views to the public good through a process of discussion; in this he refers back to the first article, which stressed "concord in the discussion of all matters."[13]

Finally, in the last article, we read: "Matters should not be decided by one person alone. They should be discussed with many others. In small matters, of less consequence, many

others need not be consulted. It is only in considering weighty
matters, where there is a suspicion they might miscarry, that
many others should be involved in debate and discussion so
as to arrive at a reasonable judgment."[14] Such then is the
finale to the kind of dialectical process that has been working
its way through the text, from its opening premise of the
overarching value of harmony and concord in discussion,
through the competing claims of truth, equally valid in themselves but seemingly in conflict, to a resolution that is more
than a static compromise but rather a dynamic process of
consensus formation.

Most of the language of the Seventeen Articles comes from
Confucian texts, and much of the reference to specific institutional arrangements draws on Chinese models, reflecting the
dialogue that has already taken place between classical Confucianism and Han institutions. The claim put in for Buddhism does not present alternative models, but only contrasting perspectives, one of transcendent faith and another of
radical skepticism. In the text itself, the evidence for linking
these to the Emptiness view is slight but unmistakable.[15] It
has, moreover, strong contextual support in the known prevalence of the Emptiness doctrine at that time, as seen for
example in the inscription on the Mandala of Heavenly Life
(the *Tenjukoku* mandala) dedicated to Shōtoku's memory by
Lady Tachibana and preserved in the Hōryūji. "This world is
empty and evanescent; only the Buddha is real." This is also a
main theme of the *Vimalakirti Sūtra,* along with the doctrine
of adaptive means. Whether or not Shōtoku is accepted as the
author of all three of the sūtra commentaries attributed to
him, the *Lotus, Vimalakirti,* and *Srimala* sūtras are known to
have traveled together through China and Korea and to have
achieved great prominence in Japan at this time. The *Lotus*
itself, as its title "The Lotus of the Wondrous Law" suggests,
preached a universal law on a spiritual plane, which could be
easily reconciled, through the principle of Emptiness and

adaptive means, to the Chinese secular law and institutions that furnished the main content of the Seventeen Articles. Indeed it was the principle of accommodation that enabled these two conceptions of law, religious and secular, to coexist in seventh-century Japan. The religious conception, with its lofty spiritual aspiration, took wings in the pagodas of temples like Shōtoku's own Hōryūji, "Temple of the Ascendancy of the Law" and numerous other temple structures that rose over the Yamato plain with the Law of Buddhism written into their names: Hōkōji, Hōrinji, Hokkiji, Hokke-ji, and so on. In due time, alongside these embodiments of the religious law came the successive codifications of the secular law that gave more precise definition, at least in writing, to Shōtoku's "exemplary law" (*kempō*).

The blending of continental ingredients in Shōtoku's confection has been summarized by Miyamoto Shōson, a leading Japanese scholar of the last generation, as follows: "The emphasis on the need of public discussions and the people's cooperation is due to the influences of the Taoist *yin-yang* reciprocal circulation principle, the Confucian principle of the Mean, and the Buddhist democratic equality."[16]

Miyamoto gives no linguistic evidence, and I would say there is none to be found in the text, for his syncretic interpretation, which is perhaps best taken as an ecumenical gesture generously sharing the credit for a popular idea while implying, as so often happens in such cases, that one's own faith (Buddhism) is more equal than others. Surprisingly left out of the account are native Japanese precedents that lend themselves to this synthesis. In documents of the same date purporting to speak for native tradition we find, as in the *Kojiki*'s account of Japan's origins, distinctly pluralistic conceptions of creation, a celebration of particularistic values, and a picture of irrepressible playfulness among the gods. Along with this there is a disposition to reconcile unruly opposing forces through the consultative process—as, for instance, when the

Sun Goddess, insulted by her brother, precipitates a crisis by hiding her light in a cave, and the "myriad deities" (*yao yorozu no kami*) consult together about how to get her to come out.[17] A similar idea is found at the ancient shrine of Izumo, said to embody the spirit of combining opposing elements (*musubi*); there the deities from the different provinces were believed to hold a congress in the tenth month of the year, each housed in its own little shrine as if in a conference circle around the main shrine (claimed by local priests as an early example of Shinto democracy!). Compare these goings-on with the opening passage of the Confucian *Book of Documents*, where the founding myth is of the sage-king Yao standing alone as a perfect personification of wisdom, dignity, and self-restraint, and one can imagine why the Japanese, not entirely comfortable with adopting such a rational, moral ideal as the basis of government, would have considered it preferable to just talk things out.

As far as democracy is concerned, it is a free world, which everyone can define for himself in his own terms, but the importance of the Seventeen Articles is better appreciated, I would say, in *their* own terms. To me it is significant that, long after the institutional arrangements projected by Shōtoku and his successors had lapsed, the process of consultation and consensus formation continued in the clan, family, privy, and party councils that have played a key role, often behind the scenes, in Japanese affairs down through the ages. Whether or not these are adjudged to be "democratic" is less important than that this so-called "constitution" proved to express the essence of the Japanese political process better than any of the legal institutions to which it might have been tied.

The Seventeen Articles are themselves a unique and distinctive product of that process, in dialogue with continental philosophies. Each of the latter had its own part to play, though Buddhism initially exerted more influence in Japan than Confucianism. Less often noticed is that the idea of their complementarity survived. This may be seen in the educational programs of the two great leaders of Japanese Buddhism, Saichō and Kūkai. With them the Confucian conception of political leadership by the wise and worthy, and for this purpose the study of the Confucian classics, remained indispensable. To the extent that a Buddhist monk as an aspiring bodhisattva would hope to render any public service, he would need to be a "wise and worthy person," a Confucian noble man.[18] And even in the heyday of the Japanese samurai, the house laws of the dominant Hōjō clan cited the *Analects* as support for the idea that consultation was essential to the conduct of human affairs.[19]

I have dwelt at some length on the Seventeen Articles because this document is so revealing of the dialogue among the major traditions in the second stage of East Asian civilizations. Nowhere else in East Asia has a document been found to compare with it. This tells us something about East Asia as well as about Japan. In lieu of such a charter the Chinese and Koreans took ancestral law as the "constitution" handed down from the founding father of the ruling dynasty—hardly a better solution. Loose and legalistically undefined though they were, Shōtoku's articles at least gave the Japanese more running room and a less cumbersome model to work with.

If my subject were simply Buddhism's adaptation to Japan, far more attention would have to be given to its accommodation to Shinto and to the emotional and aesthetic life of the Japanese, as shown in their rich literature and art. It was in this area certainly that the two religions had the greatest influence on each other. But it is in the political and social arena that their responses to each other, as well as to Confucianism and Chinese dynastic institutions, may be observed, and Shōtoku's case may perhaps serve as a convenient example of this.

In China Buddhism, linked as it was in many ways to the

fortunes of a different kind of dynasty, saw its greatest days at the height of the T'ang. The Dowager Empress Wu, effective ruler of China during the latter half of the seventh century, when Buddhism was at the height of its influence, illustrates the point well. She patronized Buddhism in ways that were consistent with her political interests and in return was acclaimed by Hua-yen monks as a universal (*chakravartin*) ruler and as an incarnation of Maitreya, the Buddhist messiah. However, usurping the throne and establishing a new dynasty of her own, she adopted the dynastic title of Chou and the Confucian name of Tse-t'ien ("one who takes Heaven as her model"), thereby confirming Confucian doctrine at least nominally, and the dynastic system more practically, as the primary source of political rationalization and legitimation. The new dynasty was short-lived, but Empress Wu remained as a model for the Koreans and Japanese of the rapprochement between Buddhism and the ruler.

Today the Great East Temple (*Tōdaiji*) and the Great Bronze Buddha (*Daibutsu*) it houses in Nara are living monuments not only to the Emperor Shōmu in eighth-century Japan but also to the Empress Wu, whose centrally administered system of provincial monasteries and nunneries Shōmu adopted. Similarly there are in Korea, near Kyongju, the Bulguksa Temple (the Temple of the Buddha's Kingdom) and the magnificent stone carvings of the Buddha and his guardian deities in the cave temple at Sukkulam, just above Bulguksa, again following the Empress Wu's example at Lung-men in China. They perpetuate the idea of the world-ruler presiding over a universal spiritual community in which the political and religious orders are mutually supportive, based on the Hua-yen philosophy of the interpenetration and interfusion of all elements of reality. But when Hua-yen speaks of the mutual nonobstruction of principle and its realization or instantiation (*li-shih wu ai*), this is predicated on the "principle" of Impermanence, Emptiness, or the Truth of

Enlightenment, and on the assimilation of all human experience into that experience of Enlightenment. Hua-yen's total acceptance of the world sees it as a theater of transworldly salvation; there is no affirmation of fixed principles to be implemented in the world as such, that is, no affirmation of defined values that could give one leverage on the political order and lead to political reform.

In practice this could mean simply the coexistence of religion and state, involving neither confrontation nor serious dialogue. Thus in the actual "rapprochement" of Buddhism and the Chinese dynastic state as it became a model for East Asia, we see a momentary accommodation of Buddhism to Chinese politics—religion legitimizing the ruler and the ruler patronizing the religion—without any genuine encounter or exchange between the two. Hua-yen Buddhism left no residual influence on the Chinese political tradition, and it is doubtful whether there was any influence in reverse.

From the late eighth century onward, Buddhism began to suffer a decline, doctrinally and institutionally, as the T'ang itself disintegrated. Another way of viewing the process, however, is to see it as a time of transition, and yes, of further adaptation to the circumstances of life in China. In this light one can observe that the great monastic institutions and schools of doctrine declined, while new forms of religious practice, deemphasizing doctrine, took their place. Of these, the practice of Ch'an (Zen) meditation and Pure Land devotionalism are the most representative of later Chinese Buddhism. In recent centuries temples and monasteries have often practiced both of these side by side. Here, however, I will deal only with Ch'an, which was to have a greater influence on the development of Neo-Confucianism in the next major phase of East Asian civilization.

Typical of the Ch'an religious ideal is the figure of the Sixth Patriarch Hui-neng presented in the *Platform Sūtra*. His story is told in the opening lines of his sermon:

Good friends, listen quietly. My father was originally an official at Fan-yang. He was [later] dismissed from his post and banished as a commoner to Hsin-chou in Ling-nan [Kwangtung]. While I was still a child, my father died and my old mother and I, a solitary child, moved to Nan-hai. We suffered extreme poverty and here I sold firewood in the market place. By chance a certain man bought some firewood and then took me with him to the lodging house for officials. He took the firewood and left. Having received my money and turning towards the front gate, I happened to see another man who was reciting the Diamond Sutra. Upon hearing it my mind became clear and I was awakened.[20]

From the same man, according to this account, Hui-neng also learned about the Fifth Patriarch, who had many followers, both lay and monastic. These he encouraged, saying "that if they recited just the one volume, the *Diamond Sūtra,* they could see into their own natures and with direct apprehension become Buddhas." Moved by this, Hui-neng went to visit the Fifth Patriarch and reported as follows:

The priest Hung-jen asked me: "Where are you from that you come to this mountain to make obeisance to me? Just what is it that you are looking for from me?"

I replied: "I am from Ling-nan, a commoner from Hsin-chou. I have come this long distance only to make obeisance to you. I am seeking no particular thing, but only the Buddhadharma."

The Master then reproved me, saying: "If you're from Ling-nan then you're a barbarian. How can you become a Buddha?"

I replied: "Although people from the south and people from the north differ, there is no north and south in Buddha nature. Although my barbarian's body and your body are not the same, what difference is there in our Buddha nature?"

The Master wished to continue his discussion with me; however, seeing that there were other people nearby, he said no more. Then he sent me to work with the assembly. Later a lay disciple had me go to the threshing room where I spent over eight months treading the pestle.[21]

There is of course more to the sūtra than this, but much of it has to do with a succession struggle that is of interest mostly to historians and not very edifying in religious terms or with doctrinal issues that tell us more about what Ch'an was leaving behind than about what it would become. The central mythic truth of the scripture lies in the story of Hui-neng himself, and the great popularity of the work in later times—what led all later schools of Ch'an to claim Hui-neng as their patriarch—was the compelling appeal of this paradigmatic figure.

From the passages quoted above one gets a quick sense of how Mahayana Buddhism has been adapted to Chinese tastes in Ch'an. Here is a new model of direct and sudden enlightenment for Everyman, as told in a down-to-earth Chinese way about an illiterate lad from the streets—poor, orphaned, disadvantaged in every way except in native wit, yet bright-eyed and bound to be a Buddha. True, the *Lotus Sūtra* had already preached the Buddha nature in all beings, and the *Vimalakirti* had shown how the bodhisattva, as layman, could be all things to all men. But Vimalakirti, with his extraordinary talents and amazing repertoire of roles and adaptive means, was more plausible as an ideal for the cultured Chinese gentry or for a learned prince like Shōtoku than for ordinary Chinese. By contrast, Hui-neng is the personification of the Chinese egalitarian ideal. He is the Buddha wearing no halo, the bodhisattva without wings, the common man sprung from the good earth of China. His story, recounted in prosaic, matter-of-fact terms as if by some local clerk in a government office, nevertheless purports to be a sūtra, the very word of the Buddha himself. Not to be mistaken for a parody of scripture, it is nonetheless a scripture to end all scriptures, a final renunciation, not of this world but of all renunciations and all religiosity not of this world.

From this point on Ch'an ceased to communicate in traditional terms and passed into essential silence, leaving behind only a few traces in cryptic *kōans* and in grudging formulations of its own teaching, as in the lines:

> A special transmission outside the scriptures,
> Not formulated in words.
> Pointing straight into the mind-and-heart
> To perceive one's nature and achieve Buddhahood.

Scripture study remained an option but, given the distrust of words, an option not often exercised. Even monastic discipline was only reluctantly committed to writing.[22] This distrust might seem an unlikely development, if one assumes the collapse by this time of any real distinction between layman and monk. But in fact the goal for both monk and layman was still enlightenment, reaching the "other shore" of consciousness, and monastic communities continued to exist as training centers for this under the authority of Ch'an masters and their lineages. For them too there remained a problem of how the life of the community was to be managed, how discipline was to be maintained and the continuity of authority assured without resort to writing. Indeed, a main motive for composing the Platform Sūtra itself was to assert—to make a public claim with regard to—the authentic spiritual succession within Ch'an. This was an issue that could not be decided simply by invoking an inexpressible experience of enlightenment.

Yet Ch'an reluctance to commit itself to words was a problem for others too, even for the government. Since exemptions from military and labor service were usually accorded to monks, the question eventually arose as to who was legitimately entitled to a monk's status and its immunities. In a country famed for its civil service exams in the classics, the idea naturally arose of accrediting monks by examining them in the Buddhist scriptures. Yet when the government was about to adopt such a proposal in 1236, a leading Ch'an master went to the Mongol chancellor to protest. Here is the record of the encounter between them:

> The Chancellor said: "I have received a holy edict to send officials to take charge of the examinations on the scriptures. Those who are able to read will be allowed to continue as clergy; and those who are illiterate will be ordered to return to the laity."
>
> The Master responded: "I am a rustic monk myself, I never look at scriptures and do not know a single word."
>
> The Chancellor asked: "If you cannot read, how could you become a senior monk?"
>
> The master rejoined with: "Is the honorable Great Official able to read [the scriptures]?"[23]

Implicit in the Ch'an master's stated position were two irreducible dilemmas: the inexpressibility of religious truth in words and the impossibility of stating who had final authority to interpret scripture. Since the government no doubt faced the latter dilemma too in finding prospective examiners, not surprisingly it decided to back off. In a face-saving formula that one would think could only come out of comic opera, or perhaps from the wildly whimsical Ming novel *A Journey to the West*, it was agreed that "the examination would take place, but no candidates would fail."[24]

After all, then, Ch'an proved in this instance to be more

equal than others. But it was only the equality of a mutual standoff, a tacit agreement to do nothing. One cannot say, it is true, that there was no dialogue, no communication at all, but what if the historical situation demanded, in pressing human terms, that something actually be done? How could one move beyond a stalemate, bridge the gap between a private experience of Enlightenment to a public consensus on political and social action? This was not early Japan, where native tradition presumably supplied some answer, either implicitly understood or reached pragmatically, to that question. It was China, and new answers would have to be found, new mechanisms and vehicles devised, in dialogue with the native traditions. This, then, brings us to a new stage of East Asian civilization.

3 | *The Neo-Confucian Stage*

IN REISCHAUER'S FIRST major scholarly contribution, his study of the Buddhist monk Ennin's pilgrimage to China in the ninth century, he characterized Ennin as "one of the last great individuals" at the end of an epoch—an epoch that had seen the expansion of Chinese civilization to the outer reaches of East Asia but that was now coming to a close with the decline of the T'ang dynasty and the persecution of Buddhism. Reischauer spoke of the ninth century as the turning point of a new phase, "a great formative period" in which would emerge most of the essential features of "the modern China with which the West came in contact in recent centuries."[1]

It is fitting that the monk Ennin should stand symbolically as the final witness to the "Buddhist Age," since it was the religious dynamism of Buddhism as it spread across Asia that had provided much of the impetus for the earlier expansionism. In the same way, if I speak of the next phase as the Neo-Confucian Age, it is because Neo-Confucianism proved to be, among the many new developments in this period, the most vital link between the "modern China" of which Reischauer spoke and the rest of East Asia. As seen from within, there may be a question about the actual depth of penetration of either Buddhism or Neo-Confucianism into any one of the cultures of the region, as compared to the persistence of indigenous traditions and their power of assimilation. Yet, from the view of East Asia as a whole, Neo-Confucianism was the primary force in shaping a new common culture, as I hope will become apparent in what follows.

As I said earlier, Buddhism was a missionary religion; its spiritual drive and zeal naturally fit the expansionist movement Reischauer describes. But Confucianism had no such proselytizing aim or apostolic mission, and one might wonder how it could generate a comparable élan. The answer, I believe, lies not only in recognizing the difference between Neo-Confucianism and Buddhism, but in seeing how the third stage of East Asian civilization differed from the second. In short, this was not an expansionist phase, but one distinguished rather by the degree of its intensive internal development—economically, socially, and culturally. In this situation, with less scope for missionaries and cultural emissaries than for teachers, scholars, and officials, Neo-Confucianism furnished the most plausible rationale for East Asian civilizations preoccupied with their own inner development—self-centered in the positive sense of being inner-directed, conservative of their energies, and concentrated in their efforts. To my mind, Neo-Confucianism is also the key to understanding how later on, in the eighteenth and nineteenth centuries, the inward-looking civilizations of East Asia would appear to the expansionist West to be ingrown, self-contented, smug, and isolationist, while the West would seem to East Asians the very embodiment of uncontrolled aggressiveness—power on the loose, bound to no moral and spiritual center.

But returning to ninth-century China, we pick up where Ennin and Reischauer left off—with the T'ang dynasty and Buddhism in decline, and new forces at work remaking Chinese society. The persecution of Buddhism that Ennin experienced in 845–846, though spectacular, need not have been in itself a fatal blow to the religion. Short-lived, and with its worst effects probably felt mostly in the capital region, the proscription only accelerated a diaspora already begun by the attenuation, institutionally and doctrinally, of the Buddhist church itself (if indeed a religion so loosely organized and lacking in any defined principle of authority can be called a church at all). Yet in spite of this seeming deliquescence, the survival of Ch'an and Pure Land Buddhism was assured in the very course of dispersion. Training and practice in Ch'an focused on the person of the Master, not on a church or parish, and the Master could be at home anywhere or nowhere. Pure Land faith looked toward the Western paradise and not to an earthly city; it was a ready recourse for the common man by what was called a "crosswise passing out" (as contrasted to a vertical ascent via the Eightfold Path), no matter what the place or time.

For both forms of Buddhism, however, the corollary of such adaptability and independence was that they remained largely disengaged from political and social concerns. In any case, they had never bid for power, only at times for patronage and protection. Offering no political philosophy, no social program, and no alternative curriculum for the civil service, and providing no remedy for the difficulties attendant on dynastic decline (except possibly personal release from them), Ch'an and Pure Land Buddhism had little or no part in the proffered solutions to these problems, which would give a different shape to the new age.

Today, after several decades of intense, specialized study of the so-called T'ang-Sung transition, it remains true, as Reischauer said earlier, that power was substantially further centralized in the dynastic institutions reconstituted by the Sung. Along with other significant changes in Chinese society, this warrants the characterization of the period as "early modern." Among the changes worth noting in this brief sketch are the further development of intensive agriculture, partly through new methods of irrigation and cultivation; the growth of industry and commerce (but with more internal than foreign trade, and a concomitant increase in the commercialization of agriculture); the use of paper money; substantial population growth and large-scale urbanization; rising affluence (subject to regional variation, but in general supporting a higher level of cultural activity, and in more diverse forms than before); and finally new technologies, both contributing to and issuing from these other advances. Our knowledge of these technological advances has expanded significantly in recent years, but for my purposes the most important for cultural growth was the spread of printing, invented in the late T'ang. Since the enduring glory of the Sung lay in its cultural products, the significance of printing as a contributing factor—both facilitating and defining the form of communication—can hardly be exaggerated. Moreover, it should be observed that these advances took place without any expansion of China's borders and, in the later Sung, within severely contracted ones.

A major feature of the new order, long recognized and still not seriously challenged, was the emergence of a new literati class, a bureaucratic and cultural elite whose leadership functions, whether in central government or on the local level, reflected a significant emphasis by the Sung on civil as opposed to military rule (without, however, any actual diminution in the pressing importance of military affairs or the great cost of the military establishment). As the Sung promoted civil rule, it encouraged relevant forms of scholarship and secular education. The monumental encyclopedia *T'ai-p'ing yu-lan* (A.D. 983)[2] expressed in its title the aspiration to achieve a golden age of civil peace and to compile for the guidance of the ruler a conspectus of all past learning. The encyclopedia typifies the governmental need for both broad knowledge and specific kinds of learning to deal with a wide range of complex problems.[3] The ambition to make such information available for ready reference was not confined to the elite, and with the availability of printing this secular learning spread, in the form of encyclopedias, manuals, textbooks, and models of many literary genres, to serve a wider readership.

Expansion of the civil service examination, a relatively open channel for official recruitment, heightened the demand for education and drew increasing attention to the need for schools. It was from the attempt to meet this educational need (a need Buddhism had no idea of filling, though it sometimes provided for its novices a basic literacy in classical Chinese)[4] that Neo-Confucianism was born. The paradigmatic teacher in the early Sung was Hu Yüan (993–1059), whose school was acclaimed as a model for the education of officials through a combination of classical study and practical learning, consisting of civil administration, military affairs, hydraulic engineering, and mathematics, from which the student chose one for specialization.[5] This meant that the new learning accepted from the beginning the need for technical specialization and was not simply for gentlemanly amateurs.

No less important than practical learning, however—and not to be taken for granted—was study of the Confucian classics, which was meant to yield the value principles for ordering and structuring the newly available mass of knowledge (the classics were not particularly featured in the *T'ai-p'ing yu-lan,* for instance). Later tributes to Hu credit him with being a particularly dedicated teacher who emphasized the "substance, function, and literary expression" of Confucian teaching. "Substance" meant the enduring ethical principles in the classics; "function," their practical application to one's own time; and "literary expression," the importance of explicit verbal communication and textual formulation. The significance of the latter is in contrast to the Ch'an Buddhist forswearing of verbal formulations (*pu li wen-tzu*) on the ground that essential truth was incommunicable. Hu's "substance and function" stressed the applicability and verifiability of Confucian principles in human life, again in contrast to Buddhist skepticism about any enduring substance or nature.

Neo-Confucians called this new kind of learning "solid," "real" or "practical" learning (*shih-hsüeh*), in contradistinction to the "empty" learning of Buddhism and Taoism. That the new learning rejected both of the latter is well known. Less often recognized is that it had an almost equal contempt for older forms of Confucian scholarship—for classical studies that were mainly philological and historical in character; for encyclopedic erudition, indiscriminately collected and lacking any evaluative criteria; and for literary composition not informed by any moral purpose.

Along with the overt rejection of Buddhism, however, went a powerful tendency tacitly to emulate its impressive spirituality. When Hu Yüan set an examination question for Ch'eng I (1033–1107), he assigned the theme "what Master Yen loved to learn."[6] Master Yen or Yen Hui was a favorite disciple of Confucius, described in the *Analects* and *Mencius* as one who, despite poverty and low station, remained blissfully absorbed in learning.[7] A cult developed in Neo-Confucianism around Yen Hui as a human ideal, someone who had come close to a beatific state of Confucian sagehood.[8] In celebration of this ideal an impressive temple to Yen Hui was erected in Chüfu, the birthplace of Confucius, during the heyday of Neo-Confucian influence. In this new religiosity of the human order we sense the unacknowledged influence of Buddhist spirituality.

The unspoken dialogue with Buddhism may also be discerned in the saying of the statesman Fan Chung-yen (989–1052) that the "noble man is first in worrying about the world's worries and last in enjoying its pleasures."[9] Some have seen this as a Neo-Confucian appropriation of the Buddhist ideal of the compassionate bodhisattva.[10] Its deeper meaning, however, lies in its response to that ideal, not in the mere imitation of it. Just as Yen Hui was to be acclaimed as a model of lofty spirituality in the pursuit of humane learning (that is, not through an enlightenment transcending human knowledge), so Fan's noble man is one who puts concern for human welfare ahead of the pursuit of his own peace of mind, relaxing only after strenuous engagement in the struggle of life. Unstated, but understood, is the reversal of the Buddhist idea that attaining enlightenment is a precondition for the bodhisattva's return to the world in order to enlighten others.[11]

This is not a trivial difference. The Neo-Confucian Ch'eng I, though obviously impressed by the training and character of individual Buddhist monks, believed that such training was not after all compatible with the kind of preparation that the Confucian conscience demanded of the noble man: moral formation in the home and community, completed by scholarly education in humanistic disciplines.

A popular syncretic formula of the day saw the Three Teachings as complementing one another, with Buddhism speaking to the mind, Taoism to physical culture, and Confucianism to human social concerns. For Ch'eng I, human experience could not be so compartmented. As paths of human cultivation, the Three Teachings, starting from different assumptions concerning the human mind, led in different directions.[12] If one spent one's best learning years lost in Ch'an meditation, one could not acquire the knowledge and experience needed to deal with pressing human problems. One had to make an early choice and a definite commitment.

A similar choice faced Chu Hsi (1130–1200), the great synthesizer of Neo-Confucianism, a century later. By that time, however, the circumstances had greatly changed. Major reform efforts in the eleventh century had failed appreciably to meliorate the nation's problems, much less remake China on the model of the ancient kings, as some Confucians had hoped. Even the most ambitious and determined of these efforts, the so-called New Deal of Wang An-shih (1021–1086), involving large-scale active intervention by the state in the economy, had been frustrated by resistance on many levels; renewed efforts by Tsai Ching (1046–1126) along the same line, including grandiose plans for a state school system,[13] came to nothing in the midst of political dissension, military defeats, and the loss of North China to "barbarian" invaders. Subsequently the Sung's survival in the south was marked by retrenchment and consolidation, a diminished role for the state, and the literati's increasing preoccupation with local rather than national affairs. It is not that the scholar elite surrendered all hope of a Chinese resurgence, but that attempts to recover the north got nowhere, and no one seemed able to mount a major reform at the center or from the top down.

As political disenchantment produced these withdrawal symptoms, some literati washed their hands of the political struggle by simply heaping the blame for their troubles on Wang An-shih and Tsai Ching. Others reacted in favor of stronger, more practical, or utilitarian methods for the organization and use of power; still others, in their disillusionment with worldly ambitions, turned back to Buddhism. Chu Hsi, for his part, sought a middle way among these alternatives, which he regarded as equally simplistic.

Though critical of Wang An-shih's basic philosophy and methods, Chu Hsi refused to blame Wang for his political activism; the human conscience would not allow one simply to "do nothing" (*wu-wei*) in the face of social evils and human distress. Indeed, contrary to the usual picture of Chu as something of a quietest or conservative, he was radical enough to assert that respect for ancestral law and precedent as sacrosanct and inviolable should not be allowed to stand in the way of basic reforms; rather, the models and principles of the sages represented a higher law to which appeal might be made in overriding ancestral law.[14] It is also true, however, that Chu himself performed little official service at court; he was much more active on the local level. His own practical efforts at reform tended to focus on specific problems of the people in his own jurisdiction—community organization and cooperative activity, improved methods of agricultural cultivation, famine relief and stabilization of grain prices, instruction in local schools, the administration of justice, and so on[15]—rather than on large-scale national programs of the type Wang An-shih and Tsai Ching had undertaken. Chu's methods were cautious and based on a thorough study of local conditions and customs, but he did not hesitate to take strong initiatives or make firm demands on local elites to sacrifice for the common good.

On a more theoretical level Chu regarded the so-called utilitarians, on the one hand, and Buddhism and Taoism, on the other, as opposing extremes: the one was short-sighted, the other too lofty and vague. The point about Buddhism and Taoism was not that they were completely otherworldly but that, having no fixed principles or criteria for evaluating and defining solutions to human problems, in the end they lent themselves to opportunism and fatal compromises with evil.[16] The difficulty with the utilitarians was not altogether dissimilar. Though less given to the high-flown idealism and diffuse sentiments of Buddhist compassion, they too lacked consistent principles based on a deep understanding of human nature, which would have enabled them to judge what was truly practical in human terms. Without such principles, the closer the utilitarians came to power, the greater the danger of their being corrupted by it.

For Chu, then, it came down to how one defined human nature and the humane values to be served by those bearing leadership responsibilities. Education was needed of a kind that would appeal to the best in human nature, which could then be systematically nurtured and trained to meet such

responsibilities. Chu himself as a young man had been powerfully attracted by Ch'an Buddhism and had even had a kind
of mystical experience.[17] Moreover, he was well aware that
other intelligent and sensitive men of his time, as well as men
of his father's and the Ch'eng brothers' generation, were
similarly attracted. Thus for him the first requisite was a deep
and thorough understanding of human motivations and how
one conceived of the self, in a way that took into account the
fundamental questions Buddhism posed with regard to both.

Virtually all of Chu's scholarly writing and teaching attempted to address this question in the broadest terms, on the
deepest levels, and in the most practical way. For this purpose, as I have explained in *The Liberal Tradition in China,*[18]
he often cited Confucius' expression, "learning for the sake
of one's self rather than for the sake of others." By this Confucius meant learning to achieve true self-understanding, not
just to win favor with others. Chu singled out this affirmative
view of the self as a way of taking issue with the Buddhist
view that the self is insubstantial and the Buddha nature
impredicable.

Of Chu's voluminous writings we know that he attached
the greatest importance to his commentaries on the Four
Books and *Reflections on Things at Hand (Ch'in-ssu lu)*. We
also know that later Neo-Confucians, following him, gave
these works the highest priority in the educational curriculum
that would dominate the East Asian scene down to the late
nineteenth century. Among the Four Books the *Analects* and
Mencius were already important in themselves, conveying as
they did basic Confucian teachings set forth in the classical
age. *The Great Learning* and the *Mean,* however, originally
chapters in the *Record of Rites,* were given new prominence
by Chu. He labored almost to the end of his life writing
concise commentaries on them, trying to achieve the utmost
clarity, precision, and economy of expression. Using philosophical language carefully, he nevertheless wrote as if to

reach the widest possible audience, not just the learned elite. Moreover, he wrote prefaces for the *Great Learning* and the *Mean* (something he did not do for the *Analects* and *Mencius*); anyone who read these primary texts would see his prefaces first, since they appeared at the beginning of most editions. If one wants to learn the basic stock of ideas that most educated men were exposed to in premodern East Asia, this is the place to start.

Significantly, in Chu's preface to the *Great Learning*, the first point he emphasized was the ruler's responsibility to provide education for all, not just by the traditional means of edifying personal example or instruction in the family setting, but quite specifically through schools maintained from the capital down to the smallest village. For him simply writing about certain ideas and values was not enough; providing tangible institutional means of schooling was also vital. Further, instruction in these schools was to be based on the principles of the *Great Learning*, using a sequence of well-defined steps and incremental stages of learning and culminating in a kind of enlightenment quite distinct from the sudden enlightenment of Ch'an.

To start with, Chu asserted three guiding principles of education. In the somewhat archaic language of the original text, the first of these was to "manifest bright virtue" (*ming ming-te*), which for Chu meant to clarify and give expression to the innate moral nature in each person. The second principle was to "renew the people" (*hsin min*), which meant to help others cultivate and express their innate good nature as the basis for the renewal of society. Here Chu follows Ch'eng I in substituting the word *hsin*, "renew," for *ch'in*, "to love, be kind to," and speaks of it as "reforming the old" rather than just expressing loving sentiments toward others. The third principle was "resting in the highest good." This meant, most immediately, striking the proper mean in dealing with human affairs, neither going too far nor falling short. In terms of self-cultivation, however, it could also mean achieving self-fulfillment through the full development and employment of one's capacities. At this point one could rest content, having acted to satisfy one's conscience rather than having sought an enlightenment transcending the moral sphere.

From these three guidelines Chu goes on to discuss the so-called Eight Steps (*pa t'iao-mu:* items, specifications), consisting of successive steps in self-cultivation, involving a range of cognitive and moral operations directed toward the goal of ordering the state and bringing peace to the world. It is, in effect, an Eightfold Path for the Confucian noble man, leading to the peace of the world, in contrast to the Noble Eightfold Path of Buddhism, leading to the peace of Nirvana.

Chu draws particular attention to the first steps in the process of self-cultivation, *ko-wu chih-chih,* most commonly rendered as "the investigation of things and extension of knowledge." He says that *ko* ("investigate") means to reach or arrive, and he indicates that this is a process by which principles in the mind are brought into contact with principles in things, and thus each is made present to the other. *Chih,* he says, is to recognize or be conscious of, to project one's knowing, hoping that one's capacity to know will be used to the full (literally, "exhausted"). The same passage can be read translating *chih* as "knowledge" instead of "knowing," but in that case it should not be understood as in "a body of knowledge," for this would set an impossible goal for the "exhausting" of learning. One would need to know everything, instead of, as he intended, simply developing one's learning capacity and understanding to the full.

Chu added a special note on *ko-wu chih-chih:*

"The extension of knowing lies in the investigation of things" means that if we wish to extend our knowing, it consists in fathoming the principle of any thing or affair we come into contact with, for the intelligent mind of man always has the capacity to know, and the things of this world all have their principles, but if a principle remains unfathomed, one's knowing is not fully exercised. Hence the initial teaching of the Great Learning insists that the learner, as he comes upon the things of this world, must proceed from principles already known and further explore them until he reaches the limit. After exerting himself for a long time, one day he will experience a breakthrough to integral comprehension. Then the qualities of all things, whether internal or external, refined or coarse, will all be apprehended, and the mind, in its whole substance and great functioning, will be fully enlightened. This is "things [having been] investigated." This is "knowing having reached [its limit]."[19]

In this passage Chu Hsi seems to be saying that if one pursues study and reflection long enough, one's understanding will be enlarged to the point where one overcomes any sense that things or others are foreign to oneself, achieving an empathetic insight that is both integral and comprehensive (*kuan-t'ung*). He will have developed his capacity for learning and knowing to its limit, and thus will be equally at home with himself and his world. At this point "learning for the sake of oneself" has overcome all distinction between self and others.

In later Neo-Confucianism great importance was attached to this holistic conception of a culminating point in intellectual and moral self-cultivation. Some later scholars saw it in an "experience" of enlightenment remarkably close to the sudden enlightenment of Ch'an; others, seeing it as consistent with Chu's philosophy as a whole, explained it as a gradual process that was indeed more than simply cognitive; without going beyond the moral and rational order, the process nevertheless had its own numinous aspect.[20]

Moreover, besides aiming at self-fulfillment, the process

would serve the second of Chu's guidelines as well. It would "renew the people" in the sense that self-cultivation, as a form of self-discipline, would better serve the purpose of reordering human society than would any form of regimentation. Here the expression Chu used was *hsiu-chi chih-jen,* "cultivate oneself and [thereby] order or govern others."[21] Most immediately this applied to the ruler or anyone who might exercise power over others, but the Chinese terms are so general as to suggest that it applies to all men. In one sense the expression parallels *hsiu-shen chih-kuo,* "cultivation of self and ordering of the state," shorthand for the combined individual and social phases of the Eight Items or Steps. But the expression is new with Chu (Ch'eng I, whom Chu followed in emphasizing the *Great Learning,* does not use it in his extant writing). Instead of simply summing up the second phase of the Eightfold Confucian path, "ordering or governing others" is to be understood in accordance with Chu's interpretation of "renewing the people"; that is, by manifesting one's own moral nature one helps others to renew theirs. The idea is that society can be governed only through individual and collective self-discipline and that collective self-reform is the means of society's renewal. It is not surprising then, that the new formula should have been spotted by later Neo-Confucians and come to be widely used, in Korea and Japan as well as China, to express the essence of a political philosophy that rests on personal initiative, responsibility, and self-discipline.[22]

Chu's Preface to the *Mean* was no less significant for headlining an important distinction Chu wished to make in his philosophy of mind. This is the distinction between the "mind of the Way" and the "human mind." The mind of the Way was something like the voice of conscience, speaking for the right principles Heaven had implanted in the mind as the goodness of man's nature; the human mind stood for the desires in man that could become selfish and opposed to the common good unless guided by the mind of the Way.[23] Chu Hsi did not speak of the human mind as intrinsically evil, but he significantly balanced the view of man's nature as good by stressing the weakness, instability, and fallibility of the human mind if it were not subjected to regular self-scrutiny, correction, and firm direction by principles in the mind of the Way.

The language Chu used to express this idea in the preface to the *Mean* came from texts of dubious authenticity in the classic *Book of Documents*. The fact that Chu, though aware of this dubiety, nevertheless drew upon these terms for this purpose, suggests that he saw them as peculiarly apt for expressing what he had in mind.[24] The sixteen characters in Chinese, attributed to the sage-king Yü, state: "The human mind is imperiled, the mind of the Way is subtle. Have utmost refinement and singleness of mind. Hold fast the Mean!" Chu further explained in the preface: " 'Refinement' means to discriminate between the two [tendencies] and not let them get confused. 'Singleness' means to hold on to the correctness of the original mind and not become separated from it."[25]

This formula was known in Chinese as *hsin-fa,* a term Chu got from Ch'eng I.[26] Its use was common to the Buddhists, Taoists, and Neo-Confucians in the Sung, though each meant something different by it. To Chu it meant at least three things: first, a message handed down from the sage-kings about the importance of mind control for the ruler; second, a method of moral discipline; and third, a standard or measure for judging men's thoughts and actions—the "measure of the mind," so to speak. That it was understood as the key to rulership is no less significant than that it could serve as a method for anyone's examination of conscience. Neo-Confucians employed diverse types of praxis to this end, two of the most common being quiet-sitting and keeping a daily record of one's self-examination. The former had an obvious resemblance to Ch'an sitting in meditation, and the latter was a popular religious practice shared with religious Taoism, Buddhism, and syncretic teachings. Though the Neo-Confucian moral emphasis contrasted with Ch'an practice, there can be little doubt that here, in praxis as in doctrine, the influence of Buddhist spirituality was being felt, reinforcing the centripetal forces converging on the self as the main pole of Neo-Confucian thought.

Rites were another subject of prime concern to Chu Hsi. He had hopes of conducting a thorough study of the classic rituals and of devising a simplified, less costly ritual for the family. He recognized that observance of the classic ritual forms designed for the ancient Chou aristocracy was beyond the means of common people and poor scholars like himself in the Sung. Nevertheless, for his efforts along this line, Chu in the end had to show only the brief *Family Ritual of Master Chu* (*Chu Tzu chia-li*) and *Elementary Learning* (*Hsiao-hsüeh*), which was largely compiled by others. Thus, even though theoretically one might say that Chu attached no less importance to rites than had the classical Confucians, in practice, unless one counts his work on community compacts, charity granaries, and so on as within the sphere of the classical concept of rites, his energies were largely preoccupied with "learning for the sake of one's self." From the *Record of Rites* he extracted for inclusion in the Four Books only the two short chapters that spoke most directly to this issue.[27]

As the Four Books with Chu's commentaries and prefaces became the core curriculum in Confucian academies during the thirteenth century, these ideas and practices spread on their own intellectual and moral merits, withstanding the official persecution of Chu Hsi and his followers just before and after his death. That Chu's teachings were backed by a fully articulated metaphysical system—of which I have said almost nothing here—no doubt recommended them to leading scholars. But this was probably less vital to the amazing progress of Neo-Confucianism than the fact that Chu had devoted so much attention to basic methods of learning and to the systematic preparation of texts suitable for education on all levels. In this respect he responded to two historic developments of his time: the availability of printing to communicate ideas and the expansion of education through the use of printing. As the spokesman for Neo-Confucianism, he succeeded in making his work both relevant and available to his age, responding to the learning needs of a new and more complex stage in the development of Chinese society. Ch'an, to be true to its self-imposed limitations, would be unlikely to engage in such an enterprise.

Yet looked at another way, Chu's consistent attention to educational needs fulfilled in significant part the early Sung reformers' aim of providing education as a way to wean the common people away from their addiction to Buddhism and religious Taoism. Moreover, Chu's emphasis on providing for the educational needs of the common man can be read as his response to the egalitarian ideal celebrated in the *Platform Sūtra*. To the extent that religion appealed to people's basic aspirations and motivations, it created a new popular consciousness. One can suppose then that the challenge of Buddhism on the popular level prompted a response from the Neo-Confucians and indirectly was a contributing factor to this advance in education.

I have said earlier that the Confucians were primarily scholars, teachers, and leaders in their home community, not proselytizing missionaries. Thus, ironically, it took accidents of history and the dislocations of war and conquest to spread the Confucian word abroad. Mongol conquerors captured the Confucian scholar Chao Fu in 1235, took him to Peking, and set him up in an academy in the capital, and from there Neo-Confucian teachings spread in the north. Later Korean princes, held hostage by the Mongols in Peking, studied Neo-

Confucianism there and eventually brought it back to Korea, where it soon became a potent force, culturally and politically. It was Japanese Zen monks, successors to Ennin as pilgrims to China, who first brought the new philosophy to Kamakura-period Japan. Korean scholars, taken as prisoners of war in the Hideyoshi invasion of their homeland, and the displaced Ming scholar Chu Chih-yü, a refugee from the Manchu conquest, completed the process of its transfer to Japan.

Neo-Confucianism has often been looked on primarily as a reassertion of Chinese tradition against foreign influences. This view is not wholly wrong, but when the Mongol conquerors adopted Chu Hsi's version of the Four Books, first as the basis for the educational system and then, after a long inconclusive debate under Khubilai, finally for the revised civil service examinations in 1313–1315, it was obviously not to reaffirm purely Chinese values but rather to acknowledge universal ones. I have discussed the process by which this came about in *Neo-Confucian Orthodoxy and the Learning of the Mind-and-Heart;* the further process of its extension to Korea is treated in *The Rise of Neo-Confucianism in Korea.*[28]

It is not possible here to say more about the impressive contributions the Koreans made to the development of Neo-Confucian ideas and institutions. When given the attention it deserves, Korea will be recognized as a most vital element in the history of Neo-Confucianism and in the civilization of East Asia. Although Reischauer appreciated this long ago, we have failed to sufficiently follow up his contribution educationally. I do wish to underscore, however, the seriousness and the wholehearted manner in which the Koreans adopted Neo-Confucianism as a complete way of life, as well as their thoroughgoing adoption of the social institutions and practices recommended by Chu Hsi—far beyond anything undertaken by the Chinese themselves.

For this overview of East Asian civilization a few key points must be made in relation to Korea. First, although Neo-Confucianism in Korea reacted against Buddhism even more strongly than it did in China, the prevalence of Buddhism during the preceding age must be seen as an important conditioning factor for Korea's reception of Neo-Confucianism. The latter built upon Buddhism in many of the same ways, conceptually and spiritually, as it did in China. Second, Neo-Confucianism nevertheless came as a new dispensation, and Koreans responded to it with many of the manifestations of a religious conversion. Third, it won acceptance among educated Koreans first as a body of learning, code of ethics, and form of spirituality before it came to be installed as a state orthodoxy or ideology. Even after being officially adopted, it continued to function as a creative cultural force and not merely as an official ritual routine. To illustrate this we might take the example of the Korean alphabet, one of the most ingenious writing systems ever devised (and particularly apt as an example because Reischauer joined in devising the accepted system of transcription for it). In its rational structure, economy of means, and functional efficiency, this alphabet of the native language demonstrated, independently of Chinese learning, how the Neo-Confucian philosophy of principle lent itself to new forms of secular learning—as testified to in the explanatory note accompanying its promulgation.[29] Similarly in the Japanese case, Neo-Confucianism, with its belief in a rational infrastructure of principle inherent in all things, was to provide a theoretical basis for the development of new forms of secular learning.[30] I am thinking here of the new forms of "practical learning" (*jitsugaku*) which appeared with the spread of Neo-Confucianism, and of which Kaibara Ekken is a good early example.

To these new developments Buddhists, in Japan as elsewhere in East Asia, offered little or no resistance; for them rational learning and secular morality were not fields crucial to salvation. Least of all would these have been contested by Zen or Pure Land teachings, which followed the intuitive, aesthetic, and emotional routes to Buddhahood and were essentially neutral as to intellectual or moral means, so long as these did not obstruct the way to the Other Shore.

In Korea the basic texts of Chu Hsi, especially his commentaries on the Four Books, were adopted as the core of both official instruction and the civil service examination system, closely modeled on that of the Mongols and later the Ming dynasty. For reasons I shall go into more in the next chapter, the system of public instruction tended to break down in Korea, as it did in China, but the Neo-Confucian core curriculum continued to function in many independent local academies. One cannot say that this was unrelated to the examination orthodoxy, yet neither can one deny that Neo-Confucian learning had its own power of attraction as an intellectual system and moral force. This becomes all the more significant in the light of the Japanese experience. The Tokugawa did not adopt the Chinese or Korean type of civil service, had no examination system, and did not maintain a nationwide system of public instruction. Yet in Japanese schools, largely autonomous and private or local in character, Chu Hsi's works served most often as the basic texts of elementary and intermediate instruction. In other words, they served as the common denominator of education in premodern East Asia, all parts of which shared in a similar process of intellectual and moral formation.

This formation, I cannot emphasize too often, was more of an orientation to life than to the world. It was centered on the self, on a self centered on the Mean. Character formation had the first priority, and bringing peace to the world, although it was the ultimate aim, was seen as impossible to achieve except through self-discipline. With this kind of life orientation inculcated by the Four Books, and with the Four Books established as the basic curriculum throughout East Asia, there is a shared outlook—or, better, a shared inlook on the human center rather than an outlook on the world at large. Culturally speaking, this might not keep the diverse peoples of East Asia from each having a different sense of self, nor even preclude a certain ethnocentrism, if not nationalism. This is illustrated by the case of Yamazaki Ansai, who, as a true Confucian, said he would have fought off Confucius and Mencius at the water's edge had they come to attack Japan; or by Yamaga Sokō, who claimed that the ruling house of Japan was the true Central Dynasty, thereby asserting the moral superiority of Japan, in Confucian terms, over the physically much larger and geographically more central Central Kingdom; or by the Koreans who thought themselves superior to the Chinese because they were more faithful to Neo-Confucian orthodoxy.[31] Nevertheless, one misses the point if one simply characterizes this introversion as ethnocentrism, since the Chinese sense of superiority was more ethical and cultural than ethnic, and a truly ethnocentric Chinese like Wang Fu-chih had a hard time even getting heard.[32]

Before concluding, I should like to return to Ming and Ch'ing China for a summary discussion of Neo-Confucian orthodoxy in its later development. In Chu Hsi's interpretation of the *Mean* (*Chung yung*), as discussed earlier, he emphasized the central agency of the mind-and-heart, and especially of the mind of the Way as the embodiment of principle in human nature. From this his teaching was known in the late Sung, Yüan, and Ming as both a Learning of Principle (*li-hsüeh*) and a Learning of the Mind-and-Heart (*hsin-hsüeh*). Then in the sixteenth century Wang Yang-ming offered a new interpretation of the mind-and-heart, emphasizing its essentially intuitive and affective, rather than intellective, character. Wang's teaching proved to be extremely appealing and indeed widely popular. Wang himself, and Lu Hsiang-shan,

to whom Wang drew new attention, both came to be officially canonized and enshrined in the Confucian temple during that same century (greatly to the horror, I might add, of
Korean Neo-Confucians loyal to Chu Hsi, who concluded
that the Chinese had gone out of their minds). It is a striking
illustration of how susceptible official orthodoxies could be
to changes in the moral and cultural climate.

Three consequences of this spectacular development
should be noted. One is that the new teaching virtually took
over the name Learning, or School, of the Mind-and-Heart
(*hsin-hsüeh*), claiming to be the true and legitimate heir to
the earlier teaching. Second, some defenders of Chu Hsi's
philosophy of mind, contesting this new claim, condemned
Wang as unorthodox and reaffirmed Chu Hsi's teachings as
the authentic Learning of the Mind-and-Heart. Others de-
spaired of rcapturing that flag and let it go in favor of rallying
Chu Hsi's adherents under the banner of the Learning of
Principle. Then, in the seventeenth century, after the fall of
the Ming dynasty, the reaction against Wang's teaching as
subjectivistic, "Buddhistic," antiintellectual and amoral was
compounded by the charge that his heterodox views, having
undermined objective learning, public morality, and the body
politic, were responsible for the dynasty's collapse.

For present purposes it may suffice to say that Neo-
Confucian scholarship, including orthodox Ch'eng-Chu
teaching, continued to embrace both the Learning of Principle and the Learning of the Mind-and-Heart down into the
nineteenth century. The former aspect fostered scholarly
study and objective inquiry, the latter aspect, moral and spiritual cultivation. As a long-term trend, there was substantial
growth in evidential research and specialized, technical study
of increasing complexity, with impressive results in many
fields of critical scholarship—enough to demonstrate that
Chinese minds had not simply been anesthetized by Neo-
Confucian mind control. Yet this intense study was still

focused on the central concerns of an inward-looking political culture, even when that focus was not on the court itself
but on the subordinate levels of the region, locality, family,
and self. Learning was in fact expanding enormously, but this
only presented new problems of integration; it did not open
up new horizons.[33]

It is well known that the Manchus reconfirmed the established Chu Hsi curriculum as the basis for official instruction
and examination. The great K'ang-hsi emperor (ruled 1661–
1722) himself took a strong personal interest in Chu Hsi's
teachings and promoted them. Lu Lung-ch'i (1630–1693)
served as the most prominent imperial adviser in pursuing
this policy. It is less well known that K'ang-hsi, adopting the
typical stance of Chinese rulers professing a benign impartial-
ity in intellectual and religious matters, avoided a hard
ideological line and was receptive as well to the views of Neo-
Confucians who minimized the differences between Chu Hsi
and Wang Yang-ming. T'ang Pin (1627–1687) is representative of this conciliatory, synthetic tendency at the K'ang-hsi
court. Despite generous intentions and liberal professions,
however, tensions remained. After K'ang-hsi's death there
was a succession struggle, and the Yung-cheng emperor, a
virtual usurper, was understandably anxious lest orthodoxy
and legitimacy be interpreted to his disadvantage. He
stretched the liberal view to the limit. In fact personally he
was much given to Ch'an Buddhism.

About midway through the Yung-cheng reign, in 1728–
29, a revolt broke out against the dynasty. Though it was
quickly put down, its leader confessed to having been inspired by the antidynastic views of Lü Liu-liang (1629–
1683), who had been a champion of the Chu Hsi revival and
a major influence on the aforementioned Lu Lung-ch'i, himself revered as a beacon of strict Chu Hsi orthodoxy in the
early Ch'ing. At this juncture the emperor had Lü Liu-liang
punished posthumously and with a vindictive thoroughness.

His remains were dug up and exposed to desecration, his family survivors punished, his writings proscribed, and numerous favorable references to him in the works of Lu Lung-ch'i expurgated. The emperor was not so lost in Ch'an meditation that he would lose such an opportunity to do in the orthodox opposition.

For the moment I leave the reader with this ironic and incongruous picture of the instruments of state being mobilized with ruthless efficiency to root out any vestiges of this orthodox Chu Hsi stalwart in the Ch'ing. It should give pause to those who have seen Ch'ing ideology and repression in monolithic terms and have made the identification of Neo-Confucianism with the Ch'ing state a fundamental assumption in accounting for China's resistance to modernization. In the next chapter I shall try, among other things, to set this matter in proper perspective.

4 | *East Asia's Modern Transformation*

IF ANYTHING CAN BE SAID with assurance about the modernization of East Asia, it is that our perspective on the process has been constantly changing. In my preface I referred to the conventional view of a few decades ago, that the modern period began in China with the Opium War of 1840 and in Japan with Perry's arrival there in 1853. If many Chinese still think of China's entry into the modern era as marked primarily by conflict with the West, it is because the Opium War still echoes in their minds as the opening gun in that encounter. More recent scholarly studies outside China, viewing the problems of modernization in a much larger time frame, have found more complex long-term factors at work in East Asia's response to the West, in light of which the dates 1840 and 1853 seem far less epoch-making.

What has probably not changed for either side is the common assumption that the key question is what response East Asian civilizations would make to the West, not what response the West would make to East Asia. Even where modernization has not simply been equated with Westernization, the progress of the West has set the norm and the pace. On this basis, then, the question has assumed different comparative forms. What did it mean that China and Japan reacted so differently to the challenge? Why was China so slow, and how is it that a civilization that had advanced so brilliantly up into the thirteenth and fourteenth century should thereafter have fallen so far behind the West and faced such enormous problems in catching up? Implicit in all these questions was the view that East Asia had to catch up with the West. Why was the question never turned around to ask: why did the West fail to keep up with the progress of East Asian civilizations?

One answer, fairly obvious, is that "progress" itself is a Western idea, and whatever the achievements of East Asians, the question would not have occurred in those terms to anyone who did not share the familiar assumption, namely, the progressive character and undoubted superiority of the West. Yet it could be asked, in slightly modified non-Western terms (in this case, the normative Neo-Confucian language of East Asia): why could the West not measure up to the civilized behavior of Confucian East Asia? Why did it not act in a mature, responsible way by getting its own house in order and staying home, as China, Japan, and Korea were doing, rather than chasing around the world to make trouble for others?

The question so put might well have occurred to readers of Lin Tse-hsü's famous letter to Queen Victoria in 1839 concerning the opium trade, for even those who would not accept the claims or pretensions of the Chinese throne reflected in that letter could still feel the force of the moral argument in Lin's opening lines:

> Magnificently our great emperor soothes and pacifies China and the foreign countries, regarding all with the same kindness. If there is profit, then he shares it with the peoples of the world; if there is harm, then he removes it on behalf of the world. This is because he takes the mind of Heaven and Earth as his mind.

> We have read your successive tributary memorials saying: "In general our countrymen who go to trade in

China have always received His Majesty the Emperor's gracious treatment and equal justice," and so on.

But after a long period of commercial intercourse, there appear among the crowd of barbarians both good persons and bad, unevenly. Consequently there are those who smuggle opium to seduce the Chinese people and so cause the spread of the poison to all provinces. Such persons only care to profit themselves, and disregard their harm to others, are not tolerated by the laws of Heaven and are unanimously hated by human beings . . .

We find that your country is sixty or seventy thousand *li* from China. Yet there are barbarian ships that strive to come here for trade for the purpose of making a great profit. The wealth of China is used to profit the barbarians. That is to say, the great profit made by barbarians is all taken from the rightful share of China. By what right do they then in return use the poisonous drug to injure the Chinese people? Even though the barbarians may not necessarily intend to do us harm, yet in coveting profit to an extreme, they have no regard for injuring others. Let us ask, where is your conscience?[1]

The "mind of Heaven and Earth" Lin speaks of at the beginning of the letter we recognize as the Neo-Confucian mind of the Way, the impartial, unselfish concern for the common good, which, according to Chu Hsi, should direct and govern the naturally self-regarding, but potentially selfish, tendencies of the human mind. We recall too that the distinction between the two had been fundamental to Neo-Confucian self-cultivation and to the doctrine of self-control as the key to all human governance. It did not rule out all trade as inherently selfish (contrary to those who have mis-read the Neo-Confucian teaching of unselfishness as denying the individual any right to the pursuit of happiness). Nor did this view, as Lin states the case, use the argument from unselfishness to disallow arbitrarily any activity deemed a threat to the state's control of the economy. Lin simply reasserted a traditional fairness doctrine, based on the Confucian principle of reciprocity or shared interest. And since this idea of reciprocity is recognizable not only as the Golden Rule in the West but also as a basic principle of interstate relations, was not Lin entitled to ask Queen Victoria, as he does at the end of the passage quoted: "Where is your conscience?"

If no more were at issue than this, one might readily concede the moral point to Lin and the Confucians. In the perspective of world history, however, one sees larger forces at work here that go beyond conditions of free or fair trade or even power relations. This was no less than a historic encounter between East Asia and the West: land-bound, agrarian China, preoccupied with intensive cultivation of the soil, self-cultivation of the person, and internal control of society, was pitted against the historically expansive West, with its roots and growth patterns established in a quite different environment. Economically the West's roots were in the maritime enterprise of the Mediterranean and Western Europe, militarily in Nordic conquests, and spiritually in the prophetic and millenarian view of the Semitic religions, whether in the Old Testament view based on the primal myths of the Covenant and the Exodus, leaving the bondage of Egypt for a promised land still of this world, or, as in the New Testament, based on Christ's command to "go forth and teach all nations." If religion was never unmixed with trade, and neither was unassisted by military power, in eighteenth- and nineteenth-century Western imperialism all three were deeply imbued with a sense of mission and fueled by a dynamism that would sooner or later bring them to East Asia. The extrovert West, impelled to break out of all limits and go beyond them to reach a providential culmination of human history, was bound to move on and determined to break into an East Asia operating on very different assumptions. East Asia received its mandate, the Imperative of Heaven, precisely as an acceptance of limits—a recognition of the conditions that circumscribe all human action and of the restraints that should govern all exercise of power or exploitation of land. I realize that general comparisons between East and West, like all assertions of "inevitability," are bound to fail, but here it seems to me we are witnesses to an almost irresistible force meeting a nearly immovable object, and the impact of the collision could not but be explosive.

In his own terms, Lin Tse-hsü was certainly right, and the case could be made for his sense of rightness that it was not mere smugness and complacency on the part of the Chinese but rather an expression of their deepest conviction—in Lin's case, convictions held at sacrificial cost, both to him personally and to China as well, if it came to that. Nor did Lin have any reason or evidence up to that point to question the correctness of the Chinese view. Why indeed should he doubt that his own dynasty had measured up to the demands of its moral mandate as well as, or better than, any other dynasty? The Ch'ing had preserved the peace of China for almost two centuries. It had not encroached significantly beyond its traditional outer limits, and yet it had provided for the support of a substantially larger population than any other country known to him or anyone else. Institutionally it had reached a maturity and stability, and culturally a refinement, that no other country could match. Moreover, in its neighbors it saw nothing to challenge these judgments. Yi dynasty Korea, accepting the same Neo-Confucian philosophy of self-discipline as the basis for governing others—"self-cultivation for the governance of men"—had preserved the peace, increased the prosperity, and enhanced the culture of its people for almost five hundred years. Japan, after retracting Hideyoshi's earlier ambitions to dominate East Asia, had learned to accept its own limits, and under the Tokugawa shogunate concentrated its efforts on maintaining internal peace and prosperity. It was a policy that yielded two and a half centuries free of both external wars and serious civil disorders (like those of the thirteenth to the sixteenth century)—an achievement impressive by any standard other than the Korean.

Some would no doubt view this seventeenth- and eighteenth-century phase of East Asian isolation in less idealistic terms, as more a defensive reaction to the advance of Western power into East Asian waters, as more inspired by xenophobia than by any love of peace, or as governed more by fear of the radical, even potentially subversive, character of Christianity. No doubt too a host of other practical considerations entered into the actual decision making. I grant this multiplicity of factors, and I do not wish to propound a monocausal view of the matter; in any case I do not consider these several factors to be mutually exclusive. But I do see the prevalence of a Neo-Confucian outlook—or, more correctly, inlook—on the world as marked by a stubborn inner-directedness, a predisposition to look inward to what was central and primary, rather than outward toward what was peripheral and secondary. If, to the West, this seemed a haughty indifference to the rest of the world or an ostrichlike isolationism, to Neo-Confucians it only gave legitimate priority to the solution of internal problems and the satisfaction of basic human needs over involvement in external ventures of doubtful benefit to the people. It was a moral and political stance grounded in the prime organic metaphor of the Neo-Confucians: the distinction between roots and trunk, at the base of the tree of life, and the branches, which could flourish only if the roots were properly cultivated.

Nor did it invalidate this position, or expose it as mere pretense, that emperors and their coteries often engaged in projects and enterprises—military, commercial, even aesthetic—that satisfied no more than their own personal predilections, power, or prestige. It remained the duty of conscientious Confucian ministers to censure such self-indulgence and remind the ruler of his primary responsibilities.

All this was manifest long before any Western threat appeared in the Mongols' reversing of their more open, internationalist policy and freedom of trade at precisely the time (1284–1320) when they were reestablishing traditional Chinese dynastic institutions and adopting Neo-Confucianism as the official teaching of the Yüan dynasty.[2] It is seen too in the Ming dynasty's pulling back from the impressive overseas enterprises of Cheng Ho on the advice of Confucian ministers like Hsia Yüan-chi, whose fiscal expertise had made such voyages possible but whose sense of internal priorities impelled him to call a halt to costly overseas ventures.[3] They had redounded to the prestige of the throne and swelled the imperial coffers, but only at the expense of the people and of sorely needed public works and at the risk of adequate defense along the inner frontier against the Mongols. In Korea the same world view translated into policies that strengthened civil government and promoted humanistic scholarship in the fifteenth and sixteenth centuries at the expense of military preparedness (which accounts in significant part for their inability to resist Hideyoshi). It is reflected further in the Tokugawa decision to consolidate its own internal control and establish a self-centered, centrally controlled foreign policy,[4] rather than pursue adventurist policies like those of Hideyoshi. For the most part these were long-term choices made without primary regard to the Western threat, and, moreover, policies of proven effectiveness as far as its practitioners could see.

Yet at this juncture in history, how far they could see became an urgent question. The classical philosopher Chuang Tzu had a good metaphor for this historical situation: the dove in the brushwood who cannot imagine what is seen by the far-flying roc, or the frog at the bottom of the well who has no idea what the larger world is like.[5] Chuang Tzu was not one to rush to moral judgment. He could see that each perspective accorded with the perceptions natural to that species. Moreover, he had a keen sense of what could happen if one failed to recognize what was natural or appropriate to each species in its own habitat. He told a parable of the fatal consequences of human do-goodism, not without some relevance to the case of Westerners' thinking to bring the benefits of civilization to East Asia. This is the fable of the Sovereign Kings of the Three Seas:

> The sovereign of the Southern Sea is called Impatient; the sovereign of the Northern Sea is called Impulsive; the Sovereign of the Center of the World is called the Primal Whole (*hun-tun*). Impatient and Impulsive met from time to time in the territory of the Primal Whole, and the latter treated them well. So Impatient and Impulsive discussed together how they could repay his kindness. They said, "All men have seven holes in their bodies for seeing, hearing, eating, and breathing. Our friend here has none of these. Let us try to bore some holes for him." Each day they bored one hole. On the seventh day the Primal Whole died.[6]

Today it remains to be seen whether or not the West's intervention in East Asia, for all our good intentions, may have similar fatal consequences. For some time now we have been drilling holes all over the earth (for oil, for nuclear wastes, for underground nuclear explosions, and so on) and on the seventh day, instead of resting, like God in Genesis I, and seeing all that we have done as good, we may well, like Impatient and Impulsive, perish with the earth. But I shall put such conjectures aside for the moment and return to the real point of Chuang Tzu's original metaphor: that both literally and figuratively the far-flying roc had it over the little dove and the frog in the well.

Lin Tse-hsü, instead of teaching Queen Victoria a lesson, learned one for himself: that what happened in the mere outpost of Canton had profound implications for the kind of

world the Chinese would live in thereafter. An orientation to
the center would no longer suffice politically and militarily;
the Chinese, and especially their leaders, would have to make
a historically unprecedented exodus into the world beyond.
Lin's awareness of this new need is documented,[7] and his
secretary Wei Yüan stressed the point further by compiling
his *Illustrated Gazeteer of Maritime Countries* (*Hai-kuo t'u-
chih*). But for his troubles Lin was driven into internal exile
and, trapped within the workings of an intractable Chinese
bureaucracy, was helpless to effectuate any change. Wei
Yüan, for his part, having no chance to go abroad, was
confined to the sort of second-hand journey one makes
through reading books and reporting what others have said
about the great world beyond.[8]

As everyone knows, the Japanese response to the same
challenge was quite different. Within fifteen years of Perry's
arrival, the Japanese moved from an initial defensive stance,
not unlike that of the Chinese, to a dynamic, outward-
looking policy that would bring Japan quickly into the West's
modern world. This process, revolutionary in every respect
except that rather than violently disrupting the national life,
it motivated a national consensus for concerted action, has
been extensively studied and reported on.[9] I confine myself
here to citing two figures symbolic of the change who bear
significant comparison to the Chinese case: Yoshida Shōin
(1830–1859) and the Emperor Meiji (reigned 1868–1911).[10]

Yoshida Shōin, the young samurai who tried to stow away
on one of Perry's ships in order to get to the West and learn
about it at first hand, was imprisoned for this violation of the
seclusion laws and later martyred for his revolutionary activities against the Tokugawa Shogunate. He became a hero to a
whole new generation, and his self-sacrifice was the spark
that fired the imagination of Japan's new leaders, many of
them his own followers. As a mythic figure for the new Japan, Yoshida manifested several tendencies in contrast to

those we have seen in Lin Tse-hsü and Wei Yüan. First, his father was a military instructor, and Shōin inherited the Bushido traditions of the seventeenth-century Confucian scholar-samurai Yamaga Sokō, a tradition quite in contrast to the civil bureaucratic and classical scholarly training of Lin and Wei. Second, Shōin was deeply imbued with the nationalistic ideology that had emerged from the fusion of Neo-Confucianism and nativist movements in the late Tokugawa period. Third, coming from a poor family with a mixed peasant-samurai-scholar background, he identified strongly with the country's grassroots and bore a deep resentment against what, to him, was the effete aristocracy of Tokugawa Japan. Fourth, as a teacher in a small local school in western Japan, Shōin symbolized a widespread local educational process that propagated the basic intellectual and moral formation of the Neo-Confucian Four Books along with native Japanese religious sentiments.[11] The influence of Ogyū Sorai, so emphasized by Maruyama Masao as a modernizing force, had already lapsed in Shōin's home town of Hagi (as it had elsewhere) by the time Shōin received his own grounding in Chu Hsi's studies, following a general resurgence of those teachings in the early nineteenth century.[12] This basic education and literacy proved a more fundamental element in the Meiji restoration and renovation than the more scholarly movements that have sometimes attracted attention in recent intellectual history.

Though well read in Chinese history and literature, Shōin was no deep philosopher, nor was he a classical scholar in the sense of the "evidential learning" that prevailed at the higher levels of scholarship in premodern China, Korea, and Japan. Like his own teacher, Sakuma Shōzan (or Zōzan), Shōin was influenced by Chu Hsi, but his chief inspirations were Mencius and Wang Yang-ming, with their emphasis on individual moral responsibility, spontaneity, and direct action. Robert Louis Stevenson, an admirer of Shōin, described him as having a "prophetic charm" and "the brave, self-helpful manner of all heroes."[13] Indeed, one of Shōin's greatest heroes was the sixteenth-century follower of Wang, Li Chih, an individualist, iconoclast, and martyr for his convictions, whose suicide in prison represented for Shōin the "mad ardor" of Wang Yang-ming (Stevenson called it in Shōin "hot, unflagging zeal"). This kind of heroic dedication Shōin saw as the essential stuff of the death-defying samurai, the *shishi* who would play such a dramatic and conflicted role in the history of modern Japan.[14] (Incidentally, this was a source of fascination also for the postwar writer Mishima Yukio, who was similarly drawn to the activist Wang Yang-ming and the kind of heroism personified by the martyred Li Chih.)[15]

In this respect Shōin was not an isolated figure. Recent studies have confirmed the strong affinity between late Tokugawa thinkers and late Ming Confucian thought (especially that of the Tunglin reformers at the end of the Ming, who, though critical of Li Chih, shared the high value he put on individual authenticity, integrity, and self-sacrifice).[16] In this light it will be a pertinent question, when we return to the Chinese case, whether such ideas or attitudes played a part in the Ch'ing Confucian response to the West, or whether the Japanese drew on the symbolic resources of Neo-Confucian tradition in ways the Ch'ing Chinese did not.

Extraordinary though Shōin's symbolic role was, it still only acted out the basic rationale for Japan's modernization put forward by his teacher Sakuma Shōzan in terms of *Tōyō no dōtoku, seiyō no geijutsu* ("the moral and spiritual values of the East, with the technical skills of the West").[17] In Shōin's determination to learn about the West firsthand, he made a significant "exodus" from the security of traditional learning. He thus prefigured the larger number of Japanese who would thereafter reach out to the West in a thoroughgoing way and in virtually all areas of Japanese life, with as yet uncertain repercussions on the core values of the tradition. Meanwhile, representing the tradition would be those "moral and spiritual values of the East" that Shōin combined in his person. As an East-West dichotomy, *Tōyō/seiyō* had a particularly Japanese quality. In China similar formulations spoke of Chinese learning or of a Way implicitly Chinese, in contradistinction to Western science and technology, without any reference to neighboring civilizations. Here *Tōyō* stood for Asia as a whole and included Japanese traditions along with the Confucian. As expressed by Shōin, this left room for Shinto, *bushidō*, national learning, and the Mito synthesis of Confucian ethics with Japanese emperor-centered nationalism.

It is at this point that the Emperor Meiji enters on the scene as a symbol of Japanese unity and of the national renovation movement—a symbol around whom Japanese loyalties and energies could be mobilized in the drive toward modernization. An unspectacular person himself, the emperor's role was similar to that of Prince Shōtoku earlier; that is, he authorized major innovations from abroad and reformulated national purposes in a new "constitution" (*kempō*), invoking the aura and precedent of Shōtoku's Seventeen Articles to sanctify a new regime. Thus, deftly and smoothly, a revolution could be accomplished in the name of tradition and renovation. As a relatively passive symbol of national tradition and consensus, the emperor stood as a counterweight to the revolutionary heroics of the activist Yoshida Shōin, helping to channel powerful emotional and religious forces in a rational, planned manner toward the collaborative construction of a new state and society. Without this balance it is unlikely that the radical changes of the early Meiji regime could have been accomplished with so little bloodshed.

The great symbolic documents of Meiji's reign are, of course, his so-called Charter Oath (1868) and the Constitution of 1889. The Charter Oath was simple and brief, like Shōtoku's Articles:

1. Deliberative assemblies shall be widely established and all matters decided by public discussion.

2. All classes, high and low, shall unite in vigorously carrying out the administration of affairs of state.

3. The common people, no less than the civil and military officials, shall each be allowed to pursue his own calling so that there may be no discontent.

4. Evil customs of the past shall be broken off and everything based upon the just laws of Nature.

5. Knowledge shall be sought throughout the world so as to strengthen the foundations of imperial rule.[18]

I shall not discuss the Meiji Constitution except to say that in my view it did fulfill many of the promises of the Charter Oath with regard to a deliberative assembly, and, though the parliamentary institutions of the Taishō and early Shōwa period were not strong enough to control the ultranationalist, revolutionary violence of the thirties, in their own limited way they did maintain the tradition of consultation and consensus down into the postwar years. Otherwise, during the war itself, Tōjō would not have been compelled to resign after the failure of his war policies (rather than carry on to the bitter end like Hitler); the diehards would not have been contained at the time of the surrender in 1945; and Japan might well have found itself a divided country like Germany and Korea.

The tradition of consultation and consensus is not, of course, the key to everything in Japanese life or to its modern success. More factors were at work than I can discuss here. Nor would I deny that the traditions symbolized by Yoshida Shōin had a significant part to play—including the tradition of direct action and even the uncompromising resistance of "heroic" figures to consultation and consensus. Marius Jansen gives apt expression to the hold Shōin had, paradoxically, on the imaginations of both of these types: "Yoshida had a tremendous hold on the next generation of *shishi*. Among his pupils were such men as Kido Kōin, Itō Hirobumi, Yamagata Aritomo, and Shinagawa Yajirō. Ironically enough, he was the particular patron saint of the men who fought against his pupils when those pupils came to power."[19] But in the final analysis I would give greater weight and credit to the consensus factor and to the tradition of adaptation and synthesis—the continuing dialogue between native and foreign elements coming down from Prince Shōtoku—for Japan's ability to meet the challenges of the modern world and maintain one of the most stable democracies in the world today.

Returning now to China, what has any of this to offer in the way of an East Asian perspective on China's modern fate? To start with, none of my observations are intended as overall comparisons of Chinese and Japanese success in modernization. With China the problems of size and mass, of historical depth and social complexity are so vast as to render any comparative judgment invidious. Nonetheless, in the modern period, for the first time in the long history of China, the Chinese have begun to compare themselves to others, and particularly to the Japanese, whose success in modernization has impressed them. If in no other way, this awareness of the outside world today clearly differentiates modern from traditional China. In other respects it is far less certain how much change has occurred. Even today China's leaders tend to explain their troubles as caused by the persistence of past practices and ways of thought (though these may appear in modern disguise).

Most students of China are familiar with the reform efforts of the so-called self-strengtheners in the nineteenth century, who undertook modernizing reforms in their own spheres of influence, often on a regional basis because effective national coordination was lacking.[20] As regional leaders forced by circumstances to rely largely on their own resources, such typical figures as Tseng Kuo-fan (1811–1872) and Tso

Tsung-t'ang (1812–1885) could easily have struck out on their own, as many earlier generals and warlords had done at a similar stage of dynastic decline, if only to make a deal with the court that would allow them a larger measure of individual autonomy. As conscientious Confucians, however, they had no such personal ambitions but only sought to contribute to a hoped-for dynastic revival. The concept of self-strengthening itself expressed a Neo-Confucian mentality, which, as we have seen, typically started from taking responsibility for coping with one's own situation, first through self-criticism and self-improvement, and then by extending one's efforts to a wider field. This attitude was common to those reared in Chu Hsi's teaching of the *Great Learning,* whether in China or Japan, as attested to by the popularity of "self-help" and "self-improvement" literature (in Japan the Samuel Smiles phenomenon). It fitted the basic Neo-Confucian political approach of self-cultivation (self-reform) as the starting point for the governance of others (*hsiu-chi chih-jen*), here applied to moral, intellectual, and material rearmament by reform leaders in China during the last half of the nineteenth century. Lacking in this attitude, however, was any clear sense of how these efforts could be coordinated and directed toward national goals; and indeed, many of their reforms were not new but drew on reform models well established in the latterday Confucian repertoire of social technologies.[21] Moreover, given their commitment to serve a non-Chinese dynasty, these leaders could hardly have appealed to ethnic nationalism as a galvanizing force.

Common to both Japanese and Chinese efforts was the disposition to reconcile Eastern and Western learning by formulas similar to Sakuma Shōzan's. In China the formulas tended toward a conservative defense of the traditional way along with a progressive adoption of modern Western learning, mostly technological at first but increasingly involving more of the Western culture that underlay and informed that technology. "Chinese learning for substance, Western learning for function" is the most familiar expression of this idea. It was easy for fundamentalist critics of this policy, like the Manchu Confucian Wo Jen, to reject what seemed to him a forced marriage of incompatible partners and to predict that, in such an inherently unstable combination, Chinese values would suffer continuing erosion to the point where the Chinese people would end up being driven "into allegiance to the foreigners."[22] Likewise it was easy for Western critics to interpret this formula as a foredoomed attempt by traditionalists to rationalize their emotional attachment to the past while making superficial concessions to inescapable realities in the present. In either case revolution would be seen as the predictable outcome of this inevitable conflict of values.

In the longer view, however, there is more to the issue than this simple juxtaposition of the facts of modern life versus a conservative defense of the status quo. Traditionalists were aware that compromise and concession had marked Neo-Confucianism since its earliest days. In the eleventh century Hu Yüan's curriculum had combined the "substance" of Confucian values with the "function" of technical specialization in mathematics, hydraulic engineering, military science, and so on—none of them subjects to which the classical Confucians had given a high priority but which the facts of life in a more complex Sung society forced later Confucians to accept. Hu's example was cited as a model by the Ch'eng brothers, who were in turn quoted by Chu Hsi in his *Reflections on Things at Hand*, by Wu Ch'eng in the great debate at the Mongol court leading to the new examination system of 1315, and by other Neo-Confucians, including Huang Tsung-hsi and Ch'uan Tsu-wang in later centuries.[23]

Chu Hsi reconciled himself to such necessities by accepting Legalist-type systems—civil service examinations, law codes, fiscal mechanisms like the evernormal granary—that had been generated from something other than Confucian "substance." And although it is true that Neo-Confucians continued to give the first priority to self-cultivation, in the Ming and Ch'ing the gradual proliferation of technical learning became recognized as relevant to "the governance of men." Indeed even classical humanistic studies had undergone technical specialization. Thus the Neo-Confucian "investigation of things and extension of knowledge" could lead to the consideration of new learning. Chu Hsi in *Reflections on Things at Hand* quoted Chang Tsai on the point: "If we handle the changing events of the world with much information, we can respond to those events about which we already know something. But if we are surprised with something unforeseen, we will be at a loss."[24] And again quoting Chang Tsai: "By enlarging one's mind one can enter into all things in the world. As long as anything is not entered into, there is still something outside the mind."[25]

But if the Neo-Confucian mind was not closed to new experience, both conservatives and progressives made assumptions about the Chinese Way, or substance, that appear questionable when compared to the Japanese case. In both cases there was a strong disposition to identify the Way with imperial rule, but in Japan the national substance (*kokutai*) referred more to a myth than to an established dynastic system—to a myth more flexibly adapted to new requirements than the cumbersome structure of dynastic rule in China. Moreover, "imperial rule" in Japan, clearly identified with native tradition, lent itself to a nationalistic ideology in ways that Manchu rule in China did not. Nationalism being one of the keys to the modern state-building process, a "Way" that lacked this potential would be seriously disadvantaged in the struggle for survival.

Likewise, in their response to the threat of force, the two revealed significant differences. In either case the inability to defend itself would tend to discredit a ruling regime, but in

Japan the damage done by Perry to Tokugawa prestige could be turned to quick advantage for nation-building by replacing an obsolete shogunate. In China, however, the absence of an alternative leadership that was both politically competent and able to draw on the symbolic resources of tradition, as were those around the Meiji emperor, meant that replacing the Ch'ing would be slower, more labored, and in the end more traumatic to tradition.

The Manchu regime, though, had to cope with even more serious disabilities. The case for preserving the traditional Way relied heavily on the presumption that, if the leadership acted vigorously to win or keep the hearts and minds of the people, traditional values could be counted on to preserve the solidarity of the Chinese people and strengthen their will to resist. Yet here a fatal weakness revealed itself in the questionable claim of the establishment, the Ch'ing dynasty, to represent tradition. It is not so much that the Manchus were non-Chinese, since the tradition—in contrast to modern nationalism—was more universalistic than ethnocentric. It was rather that the Ch'ing had come to power as a conquest dynasty; yet, as a tiny ruling minority in a vast sea of Chinese, it relied more on a pacific Confucian ideology and the ideal of the self-controlled gentleman than on the size of its garrisons to maintain its authority. Thus in meeting its nineteenth-century crisis, with its power and prestige now seriously damaged and without the appeal to nationalism as a line of self-defense, the Ch'ing rulers also were in a questionable position to rest their case for Chinese support on a purely traditional ground. Whether they had ever "won the hearts and minds of the people" in this idealistic or ideological sense remained in doubt.

It is true that by the nineteenth century Chinese resistance to the Manchus had ceased and there was general acquiescence in Manchu rule, with Confucian scholar-officials increasingly disposed to identify their own interests with those of the dynastic state. Thus, as Benjamin Schwartz has said, "For the bulk of the literati the preservation of the faith and the preservation of the state were indivisible."[26] Yet Yen Fu, in a memorial of 1898, exposed another facet of the problem when he said, "There can be no Way without a state and a people to sustain it."[27] Here the people's ability to sustain the dynasty and meet the modern test as the Japanese had done involves questions about the tradition as well as about the Manchus.

For one thing, in the given circumstances there was a problem about the means for reaching the "hearts and minds of the people." The geographic and demographic problems were of immense scale if popular sentiment and support were to be mobilized as the Japanese had done in a far more compact and homogenous society, one that afforded much more rapid communication and effective coordination of effort.

The issue goes back to one of the great unfulfilled promises of the tradition itself; the Chinese had persistently failed to achieve the system of universal schooling that the great Neo-Confucians, especially Chu Hsi, had insisted was the sine qua non of winning the minds and hearts of the people (originally, away from Buddhism and religious Taoism). Generations of Neo-Confucian scholars had drawn attention to this failure and had urged their contemporaries to remedy it. Many saw the failure as stemming from the inclination of dynastic regimes to treat education mostly as a device for recruiting talent into the bureaucracy, to the neglect of the people's general education, which Chu Hsi had said must be the primary aim. Nor was this true only of independent reformers like Ch'en Hsien-chang (1428–1500) and Huang Tsung-hsi (1610–1695), who were far removed from the halls of power. Even the leading Ch'ing Neo-Confucian custodian of the orthodox record, Chang Po-hsing (1652–1725), highly placed at court but still frustrated in trying to change things, registered the same complaint in drawing renewed attention to Chu Hsi's views.[28]

The historical reasons for this impasse are complex and difficult to evaluate. It would be easy to fix the blame on the exploitative and repressive features of dynastic rule in general, and in particular on its short-sighted view of education as primarily a vehicle of official recruitment. Another highly plausible explanation would be that in an agrarian society the predominantly peasant population had little use for the kind of classical learning featured in the schools and little time to spare for it in the hard struggle for existence. Yet this in turn brings us back to the question of high culture versus low culture. I do not mean to posit a sharp break between the two or to conjure up the old specter of mandarin China segregated into an educated elite and an illiterate peasantry, a stereotype increasingly brought into question by more recent studies.[29] It remains true nonetheless that the dominant form of Confucian classical education—actually neoclassical and Neo-Confucian in the Four Books curriculum—had a distinct orientation toward the training of scholar-officials; in fact, virtually all segments of the population, and not the state alone, took for granted that the only real goal and reward of education was the gaining of official preferment, a privileged status limited to a select few.

It is true that Chu Hsi had tried to reach out further to a wider audience and for larger educational purposes. It is even more relevant that Wang Yang-ming's revision of key Chu Hsi doctrines, prompted in part by what he saw as an overly bookish, pedantic, and literocratic approach to learning, attempted to redefine learning in terms more meaningful to the common man. The results were indeed spectacular, and for a time Wang exerted a powerful energizing effect on a broad spectrum of Ming popular culture. If this nevertheless proved short-lived, it is probably owing to more than conservative opposition and, later, official disfavor. Wang himself failed to produce a set of primers and texts that would serve the educational needs of this larger audience better than Chu's Four Books. As a result Chu's more methodical, scholarly approach prevailed and continued to set the direction for East Asian education.

In this outcome the very strength of the scholarly tradition reasserted itself. The most militant counteroffensive to Wang's ideas was mounted by Ch'en Ch'ien (1497–1567), whose *General Critique of Obscurations to Learning* (*Hsüeh-pu t'ung-pien*), begins with a startlingly frank assertion of Ch'en's basic premise: "There is nothing greater under Heaven than scholarship, and no greater calamity for scholarship than obscuration of truth."[30] The failure to make clear conceptual distinctions, Ch'en argues, leads to a confusion of issues between Chu Hsi's teaching and that of Wang Yang-ming and Lu Hsiang-shan. According to Ch'en, Lu's and Wang's method of self-cultivation aimed at "nourishing the spirit," reflecting the subtle influence of Buddhism and Taoism, whereas Chu Hsi's aimed at scholarly study and discursive analysis, emphasizing concrete facts, things, and affairs. Ch'en quotes Hu Chü-jen: "Confucians nourish the Way and principles; Buddhists and Taoists nourish the spirit."[31]

Whether Ch'en is entirely right in his characterization of the opposing positions, we are not wrong in seeing here a drawing of lines with significant long-term implications. Seventeenth- and eighteenth-century Confucianism would move in the direction of an increasingly rationalistic and positivistic scholarship, while distancing itself from things of the spirit, which meant cutting itself off further from some of the springs of popular religious inspiration and moral dynamism.

If we compare this to the Japanese case, we find that there too "orthodox" Neo-Confucians like Yamazaki Ansai and his school were aware of Ch'en Chien's strictures and yet declined to follow the Ch'ing trend toward the estrangement of scholarship and religion. The latter continued to play a significant role alongside Confucianism (Buddhists teaching the Four Books in village schools), often in direct collaboration (the frequent syncretism of Neo-Confucianism and Shinto in Tokugawa thinkers, the fusion of Confucian ethics and native religious traditions in the *kokutai* ideology, and so on).

In this comparative light we might ask, even while acknowledging the impressive achievements of Ch'ing critical scholarship and evidential inquiry, whether on the political level these cultural refinements were not offset by the loss of new growth at the grassroots, as Confucianism became cut off from the popular religious sentiments to which, in Japan, Yoshida Shōin had so appealed. If that was the case, it may be that Ch'ing Confucianism, given this secular orientation, also allowed itself to become too closely associated with the dynastic state.[32] Such an alliance, natural enough but not without its own risks and liabilities, could prove even more fateful in view of that state's failure to cultivate by educational means what Yen Fu had seen as equally vital: "a people to sustain it." Christian missionaries in late nineteenth- and early twentieth-century China, noting this educational lack and seeing it as an opportunity, moved in to fill the gap—to the further consternation of conservatives like Wo Jen.

In contrast to the relatively uncoordinated and piecemeal approach of the self-strengtheners was the comprehensive program of K'ang Yu-wei during the "Hundred Days of Reform" in 1898, which may be taken as transitional to the revolutionary programs of Sun Yat-sen and Mao Tse-tung. K'ang's program was visionary, prophetic, and, as articulated in his *Book of Grand Commonalty* (*Ta-t'ung shu*), total. Utopian in many ways and incorporating distinctly nontraditional elements, his thought, in its scope and sweep, went far beyond the more modest reformism of the self-strengtheners. Yet one may ask whether, in some essential respects, it did not remain within the orbit of Chinese tradition.

Although K'ang was to pick up important concepts from the West, his conception of himself and of his role in life was already well set in his early Neo-Confucian formation. He had an intense belief in himself as a sage with a heroic vocation to save the world.[33] K'ang identified strongly with Wang Yang-ming and Lu Hsiang-shan,[34] and early in life he had had a mystical experience while he practiced quiet-sitting. "All of a sudden I saw that Heaven and Earth and all things were of one substance with myself, and in a great release of enlightenment I beheld myself a sage and laughed for joy; then suddenly I thought of the sufferings and hardships of all living beings and wept in melancholy."[35] From this and other early learning experiences remarkably reminiscent of Ming Neo-Confucians like Ch'en Hsien-chang and Wang Ken,[36] K'ang derived a powerful conviction of the rightness of his cause, exuding a dogmatic self-assurance and confidence in his own opinions that stayed with him throughout life. He thus drew on the same prophetic strain in Neo-Confucian thought as Yoshida Shōin, though not on the other symbolic resources available to Shōin in the Japanese tradition.

Most modern interpreters of K'ang, impressed by his later repudiation of Ch'eng-Chu Neo-Confucianism, which they consider only an outworn scholastic tradition, have failed to recognize this prophetic role as no less typical of the tradition as a whole and not simply of its so-called Lu-Wang school. I have discussed the importance of this prophetic strain under several headings elsewhere, including its vital connection with the "tradition of the Way" or "succession to the Way" (*tao-t'ung*).[37] Key features of this prophetic, fundamentalist repossession of the Way were its repudiation and abrogation

of intervening "tradition" as corrupt, its substantial rein-
terpretation of the classics, and its revisionist view of history—all characteristic of K'ang's thought as a whole.

As further confirmation of the central place this prophetic
role held in Neo-Confucianism and of its relevance to K'ang,
I revert to the case of Lü Liu-liang (1629–1683), cited in Chapter 3. Lü, we recall, was the prime champion of the orthodox
Ch'eng-Chu revival in the early Ch'ing, who swept aside as
perverted all Neo-Confucian thought after Chu Hsi and saw
himself as the only authentic interpreter of Chu in almost five
hundred years.[38] Moreover, Lü's radical, fundamentalist attack on dynastic rule was the inspiration for the Tseng Ching
rebellion in 1728. Although K'ang himself may not have
been fully aware of the significance of Lü in later Ch'eng-Chu
thought, Lü's case is a reminder that such radical revisionism
was not new, that it had a certain potential, at least conceptually, for a revolutionary transformation of the established
order, and that, if K'ang himself is to be seen as "revolutionary" in his own thought, it must be for other new elements
proclaimed through this prophetic role.

Among the many non-Confucian elements in K'ang's synthetic thought and political program, two have a special
meaning here. By 1898 many reformers had become intensely
conscious of the need to do something about education. It
was a sign of the times, however, that K'ang, in calling for a
system of national schools that same year, cited the success of
foreign examples like Prussia and Japan, not native Chinese
precedents. Whether or not his highly selective reading of
either Chinese history or Neo-Confucian thought allowed
K'ang knowledge of these earlier attempts, for him in this
late stage of crisis precedent alone counted for little, and a
record of past failure counted for even less.

By whatever route, K'ang and his colleagues had become
aware of the urgency of the problem, yet the manner in which
they dealt with it showed not only an incomprehension of

earlier failure but a typical disposition on the part of scholar-officials to make the same mistakes. As Hsiao Kung-ch'üan recounted (not unsympathetically):

> To expedite the development of a school system in the provinces, K'ang suggested that the traditional academies (*shu-yüan*) be converted into "middle schools" and the buildings of "unauthorized shrines" (*yin-tz'u*) be used to house elementary schools, which all children six years old should be required to attend. Middle schools should have "Western subjects" in their curricula. K'ang cited the example of Meiji Japan to support his argument. Thanks to modern education, which gave her leaders knowledge in Western government, literature, and technology, the island country was strong enough to defeat China in War. In a decree issued on July 10, the emperor adopted his suggestions without reservation.[39]

That nothing would come of K'ang's reforms in any case was ensured by his political ineptitude at court, and yet a certain naiveté shows itself in this instance as well. Merely taking over existing private academies and religious schools and converting them, mostly in name, though only a temporary expedient, was typical of the short-sighted measures of earlier reformers. It reflected a persistent indisposition to address in any systematic and thoroughgoing way the actual problem of resource allocation in support of such a major undertaking. No doubt this indisposition was nourished by Neo-Confucian habits of mind favoring self-sufficiency and autonomy. These in turn justified a laissez-faire policy at court, leaving local government on its own to mobilize resources for local needs, while licensing the court to promulgate ideal prescriptions and rationalistic plans that often failed to come to terms with fiscal realities on the local level. Like the disarming of the nation militarily (as shown in the preference for dealing with security problems on a decentralized basis through local militia),[40] this predisposition toward fiscal and military decentralization disarmed the dynastic state, even though it was a centralized bureaucracy, and kept it from acting like a modern nation-state. From a modern point of view the public philosophy and dynastic system pulled in different directions and often worked at cross-purposes.

K'ang Yu-wei attempted to finesse this difficulty by simply exploiting locally available resources (themselves developed by local, "private" initiative in the wake of the state schools' failure to perform on earlier promises). All the while one could congratulate oneself for "saving the world" by doing nothing more than having the emperor grandly, magnanimously, and "without reservation" hand down yet another paper decree mandating reform.

It is here that we see Neo-Confucian idealism at its romantic worst, often celebrating its utopian dreams in "heroic" self-congratulatory verse, while assuming as always that conscientious officials down the line would find a way to live up to the norms set at the top. K'ang Yü-wei, though representative of that type of reformism known as "pure criticism" (*ch'ing-i*), which sought to rouse scholar-officials to urgent action, still assumed that the problem was to get the ear of the court and set a direction—an example of leadership— from the top down.[41] His "criticism" and exhortation are addressed primarily to his own class of scholar-officials. Thus, while performing like Yoshida Shōin in the Neo-Confucian role of hero and prophet, K'ang addresses an elite audience that, for the most part, functions in collaboration with an imperial bureaucracy that has become an end in itself. The thought of working from the bottom up, not the top down, by activating and mobilizing "grassroots heroes" like Shōin's, hardly occurs to him except as something very Japanese.[42] But then, not all prophets are both visionaries like K'ang and heroic activists like Shōin.

Such was the kind of unrealism that allowed many of
K'ang's best insights to evaporate into the thin air of utopian
plans and arcane irrelevancies. Another example is his per-
ception that China desperately needed the unifying symbols,
moral energy, and social discipline of religion, a view that
underlay his highly contrived attempt to establish Confucianism as a state cult. No doubt this sprang from a deep and
most sincere conviction, since K'ang himself had manifested
such a mystical devotion to Confucius, whether by identifying himself with the Master or the Master with himself. Yet
his conviction was also compounded of a sense that in both
the West and Japan religion represented a powerful unifying
force. K'ang was impressed by the dynamic *kokutai* ideology
of Japan; although *kokutai* was not directly transferable to a
China without Shinto, he applied the kindred idea of a "national essence" (Japanese, *kokusui;* Chinese, *kuo-tsui*) to
Confucianism.[43] Because it was implausible to rationalistic
Confucians and unacceptable to liberated progressives, however, Confucianism as a state religion came to nothing.

Neither of these ventures, in education or religion, lends
itself clearly to categorization as "traditional" or "modern,"
for in each K'ang strained to bridge two worlds—Confucianism and nationalism, monarchism and egalitarianism. In
the arena of history, however, K'ang's views had revolutionary implications for China. The point is not so much how he
rewrote past history as how he projected a new future—an
indication of the profound impact on K'ang and his generation of the Western ideas of progress and evolution.

The full meaning of this tidal change in Chinese thinking
will not be apparent to those who merely see this new "future" in contrast to a tradition identified with the past. In
truth that tradition had always been more oriented to the
present that to the past; in other words, it invoked its pasts
selectively to serve present purposes. As Chang Kwang-chih
has said of the earliest historical writing in China:

It appears that by Eastern Chou times there had evolved a standard generalized history of the previous fifteen hundred years, and that the behavioral patterns evident in this history enabled men of learning to foretell the future.

The ability to predict was, of course, the central purpose of the traditional historiography of China. To the question "Why was the study of the past so esteemed and what sorts of value were ascribed to it?" Arthur F. Wright gave the following answers: "One is that the successes and failures of the past provide sure guidance for one's own time . . . The Confucian tradition, as it developed, perpetuated the injunction to study the past as a repository of relevant experience."[44]

Here even Chang's references to the "future" have to do with the immediate future and how to deal with present problems. No future is projected on the basis of an evolution from the past. Rather the value of the past lies in its similarity to the present, and the predictability derived from study of the past lies in the constancies in human affairs, in history repeating itself, so that the paradigmatic actions of the Sages can be models for the present.

Similarly with Taoism and Buddhism. Both Lao Tzu and Chuang Tzu had taught what Lin Yutang later rendered as "The Importance of Living," that is, living in the present. As found in Chinese Buddhism, the past had little meaning in the Confucian sense, but if there is any significance to its "Chineseness" in either of its dominant forms—Ch'an or Pure Land—it lies in their addressing the present condition of man, the here and now of Ch'an and the "crosswise passing out" (rather than the long slow ascent to Buddhahood) in the Pure Land faith.

For Chu Hsi, too, history and tradition both focused on what was "near at hand," or how an understanding of the

Sage's Way could bring self-fulfillment in the present. In the *Liberal Tradition in China* I have remarked on the frequent use of the term *hsin* ("new," "renew," "renovation") in the Sung period by Confucians of many political stripes, whether in the New Measures (*hsin-fa*) and "New Interpretations" (*hsin-i*) of Wang An-shih; the "new rituals" of Ch'eng I, Ssu-ma Kuang, and Cheng Chü-chung; or the "renewing of the people" in Ch'eng I and Chu Hsi. Even "Restoration of the Ancient Order" (*fu-ku*) was used as a slogan to sanction institutional innovation, while the Way of the Sages was converted into a practical way to Sagehood for everyman to follow in contemporary circumstances.[45]

All of these expressions grew out of a belief in the Way as life-renewing, expressed in the terms of the great appendix to the Book of Change (*I-ching*) as *sheng-sheng*, with a primary analogy to the organic cycle of biological life renewal. They did not forecast progress into a future assured by any cumulative historical process, or any exodus from present bondage into a promised land. The appeal to precedent and past authority did indeed confirm a continuity in certain values from past to present as the warrant for reform, but reform was seen as serving urgent present needs rather than as leading to an ever-improving future.

If the future loomed at all in the consciousness of most people, it was as the perpetuation of the family, an extension of its continuity with the past. Politically, this strong consciousness of perpetuating the life and fortunes of the family translated into the ruling family's concern for preserving the reigning dynasty. Here, however, perpetuation became a protective, defensive concept, strongly associated with observance of dynastic precedent as the source of a ruler's inherited claim to sovereignty. As we have already observed, in Ch'ing China this tended to weigh heavily as a drag on reform, in contrast to the Japanese situation in which the misty origins of the imperial house, along with its effective isolation for centuries from actual rule, meant that it was largely unburdened with detailed political precedents.

The problem was not an entirely new one for the Chinese. Both Huang Tsung-hsi and Lü Liu-liang in the early Ch'ing, as leading spokesmen for the Wang Yang-ming and Chu Hsi schools, respectively, had insisted that there was a fundamental difference between the familial relationship, which was natural and inescapable, and the consensual relationship of ruler and ruled.[46] But when K'ang Yu-wei drew on a past idealized as the Grand Commonalty and turned it around to serve as the symbol of a utopian future—the irresistible outcome of a universal "evolution from Disorder to Order, and from Order to Great Peace"[47]—he was not only asking the Chinese to view their history in a fundamentally different and Western way. Indeed he was—more perhaps than his imperfect understanding of the West or even his idiosyncratic reading of the Chinese past allowed him to realize—calling upon them, with the voice now of a Western prophet, no longer to linger in bondage to a dismal present, but to make an exodus that would turn the present into an Advent.

Sun Yat-sen, far more influenced by Western attitudes even than K'ang, was a revolutionary in this same sense of projecting a Grand Commonwealth of the future in the name of the ancient ideal of *T'ien-hsia wei kung* ("all under Heaven shared in common"). But recognizing that monarchical rule in the established Chinese form was incompatible with progress toward this ideal, he promoted a republican revolution, not just a new evolutionary process. Even so, he encountered stubborn obstacles to getting out of the present Chinese condition. The Manchus had indeed collapsed in 1911, but more because of the dynasty's internal weakness and the penetration of its soft Confucian underbelly by liberalizing reforms in the decade before than because of concerted attack by any organized revolutionary force. Thereupon the inability of the Chinese to reestablish an effective central government convinced Sun that they were resistant to nation-building. They were, he said, "a sheet of loose sand,"[48] lacking all national cohesion. This condition he attributed to an excess of individualism and to a loyalty centered on the family rather than the nation. Hence his struggle for liberation started from a present condition of excessive particularism, on the one hand, and a diffuse, cosmopolitan universalism, on the other, to achieve the mean in the "freedom of the nation."[49] To bridge this anarchic present and lead to a democratic future, party tutelage was his answer to the popular expectation of instantaneous, full-blown democracy as the immediate realization of the ideal. His Three Stage theory, unlike K'ang's Three Stages of historical evolution, was a program of revolutionary political action for a generation whose rising expectations could not wait for evolution. It would take, he calculated, just nine years to complete the process.

That revolutionary expectation is perhaps nowhere more rhapsodically expressed than by Li Ta-chao, later to be acclaimed as a cofounder of the Chinese Communist Party, when he hailed the victory of the October Revolution in Russia in 1918. Intoxicated with the thought that the millennium was at hand, he spoke of the Bolshevik movement in euphoric terms:

They hold that all men and women should work. All those who work should join a union and there should be a central administrative soviet in each union. Such soviets then should organize all the governments of the world. There will be no congress, no parliament, no president, no prime minister, no cabinet, no legislature, and no ruler. There will be only the joint soviets of labor, which will decide all matters. All enterprises will belong to those who work therein, and aside from this no other possessions will be allowed. They will unite the proletariate of the world, and create global freedom with their greatest, strongest power of resistance: first they will create a federation of European democracies, to serve as the foundation of a world federation. This is the ideology of the Bolsheviki. This is the new doctrine of the twentieth-century revolution.

In a report by Harold Williams in the London *Times,* Bolshevism is considered a mass movement. He compares it with early Christianity, and finds two points of similarity: one is enthusiastic partisanship, the other is a tendency to revelation. He says, "Bolshevism is really a kind of mass movement, with characteristics of religion" . . . Not only the Russia of today, but the whole world of the twentieth century probably cannot avoid being controlled by such religious power and swayed by such a mass movement.[50]

Note especially that in the midst of this ecstatic vision Li himself is conscious of it as a religious phenomenon, a new faith bringing almost instantaneous salvation. If, however, the intellectual Li Ta-chao thus saw the revolution as so near at hand, bringing the future within easy reach of the Chinese, Mao Tse-tung's sense of the situation in 1927 was more sober, practical, and, in a way, far-seeing. On the basis of his observation of conditions in Hunan, he saw the peasant masses as constituting the main force of revolution. This did not mean, as some have assumed, that peasants would lead the revolution, but rather that whoever thought to lead it would need a keen sense of the peasants' present problems, as well as of the potential power that could be generated if peasants were properly led. Mao was already skeptical that Western-educated Chinese were fitted for this. His doubts emerge in comments on "foreign schools": "The 'foreign-style schools' were always unpopular with the peasants. In my student days I used to stand for the 'foreign-style schools' when, upon returning to my native place, I found the peasants objecting to them. I was myself identified with the 'foreign-style students' and 'foreign-style teachers,' and always felt that the peasants were somehow wrong. It was during my six months in the countryside in 1925, when I realized I was mistaken and that the peasants' views were right."[51]

From this one can see that Mao's basic insights into the nature of the revolution contrasted sharply with Li Ta-chao's internationalist and utopian ideals. Mao's views came from experiences no less typically Chinese—the kinds of practical lessons learned from those who worked the land, with virtues and strengths that sprang from the soil and from centuries of peasant labor, frugality, self-help and mutual aid, the struggle to survive—the hard realities of Chinese life for ages past, from the true center of the Central Kingdom.

These were the same strengths Mao relied on in undertaking the Long March to the West, which was to become the great epic of the Chinese Communist revolution and its central myth, embodying those revolutionary qualities and heroic achievements recalled thereafter, again and again, as the enduring values of a continuing revolution. Epic "exodus" though it was, however, this journey led not to the new horizons of the Western world but further into China's interior, in fact to the ancient homeland of Chinese civilization, where even the caves of Yenan—home base for Mao and his comrades—spoke of a hardy way of life lived close to the good earth. In a sense this was Mao's heroic equivalent to Gandhi's epic March to the Sea, where the making of salt would symbolize the Indian people's self-sufficiency, reliance on moral and spiritual values, and struggle for self-determination. The difference is that Gandhi had had an extensive Western education and was able to challenge Western power on its own moral and legal ground. Mao had not studied abroad, knew no Western language well, and was limited in his knowledge of the outside world. Though in some ways a doctrinaire Communist, his sense of Chinese Communism was mostly

Chinese, including even his appropriation of Marxism-Leninism-Stalinism to a native concept of ideological succession to the Way (*tao-t'ung*) which left room for his own prophetic role. Even today the patriarchal portraits of Marx, Engels, Lenin, Stalin, and Mao hang together in public displays of the prophetic succession.

While drawing heavily on indigenous moral resources and authoritarian traditions, Mao's doctrine of protracted struggle powerfully affirmed its unprecedented historical significance by emphasizing revolution as a total liberation from the past. Thus the victory won in 1949 by the People's Liberation Army was to be known for all time as the "Liberation," with pre- and post-Liberation marking a historical watershed comparable, as a decisive moment in time, to the turning point from B.C. to A.D.

That significance is further underscored by Mao's simultaneous rejection, in his tract "Combat Liberalism," of the principal alternative to revolutionary "liberation." Liberalism, to him, stood for any compromise with established practice, any relaxation of principled revolutionary struggle because of a bourgeois instinct for peace at any price or because of a weak self-indulgence in sentimental feelings for others.[52] If we compare this attitude to the moderate, gradualistic approach in which reform is seen as growing organically out of the past or as building on a clear-eyed assessment of the present, we can recognize how Mao's insistence on such a radical break—on "liberation" as a relentless campaign of liberation *from* a totally unredeemable present, rather than *toward* a well-defined future—set his "liberation" poles apart from reformist "liberalism." Immediate action, not a well-worked-out, prudential program, was what was needed to overthrow an existing order already condemned as totally corrupt. In this light liberation, seemingly so emancipated, yet so carried away by its moral fervor and blinded by its rapt vision of dawning glory, remained unconscious of the heavy burden it bore from the past.

Among the more educated comrades, brought up like Mao on the Four Books and Neo-Confucian moral discipline, Neo-Confucianism still served as a basic frame of reference for the party elite, who were to hold themselves to a higher standard of responsibility and rectitude. Liu Shao-ch'i explained this in his training manual, *How to be a Good Communist:*

There should be different kinds of methods and forms of cultivation. For example, many of our comrades keep a diary in order to have a daily check on their work and thoughts or they write down on small posters their personal defects and what they hope to achieve and paste them up where they work or live, together with the photographs of persons they look up to, and ask comrades for criticism and supervision. In ancient China, there were many methods of cultivation. There was Tseng Tze who said: "I reflect on myself three times a day." The *Book of Odes* has it that one should cultivate oneself "as a lapidary cuts and files, carves and polishes." Another method was to "examine oneself by self-reflection" and to "write down some mottoes on the right hand side of one's desk" or "on one's girdle" as daily reminders of rules of personal conduct. The Chinese scholars of the Confucian school had a number of methods for the cultivation of their body and mind. Every religion has various methods and forms of cultivation of its own. The "investigation of things, the extension of knowledge, sincerity of thought, the rectification of the heart, the cultivation of the person, the regulation of the family, the ordering well of the state and the making tranquil of the whole kingdom" as set forth in *The Great Learning* also means the same. All this shows that in achieving one's progress one must make serious and energetic efforts to carry on self-cultivation and study. However, many of these methods and forms cannot be adopted by us because most of them are idealistic, formalistic, abstract, and divorced from social practice. These scholars and religious believers exaggerate the function of subjective initiative, thinking that so long as they keep their general "good intentions" and are devoted to silent prayer they will be able to change the existing state of affairs, change society, and change themselves under conditions separated from social and revolutionary practice. This is, of course, absurd. We cannot cultivate ourselves in this way.[53]

Liu goes on to emphasize the need to "combine the universal truth of Marxism Leninism with the concrete practice of the revolution" in the context of party struggle and group discipline. Nevertheless it is clear that he wished not to lose the spur to selfless action represented by traditional self-criticism and moral discipline. Neither Liu nor Mao can be called Confucians, or anything but avowed Communist revolutionaries, yet their brand of Communism appealed to a powerful strain of moral idealism with deep roots in Chinese culture.

Even further removed from Neo-Confucian learning in his intellectual outlook, Mao continued to insist on revolutionary morality as by far the most important element in education, to the point that he and his comrades in the Cultural Revolution allowed China's schools to be closed for years and, when they were reopened, allowed only peasants, workers, and soldiers to be teachers, not trained scholars. The real meaning of the Cultural Revolution, then, was that it preached a "naked morality" stripped of all culture and learning, whether Western or Chinese—shorn of anything that was not gained from revolutionary experience yesterday or today. To the rest of the world the closing of schools and the innumerable reenactments of the Long March by zealous Red Guards seemed utterly bizarre and irrational; to Mao and the leaders of the Cultural Revolution, however (whatever their political motives and their manipulation of the movement for their own ends in the continuing struggle for power), these demonstrations served to rouse the individual moral will and recreate a revolutionary élan.

Drawing heavily, as it did, on a simple version of the Chinese sense of practicality and moral self-sufficiency, the Cultural Revolution could also be seen as a throwback to the old idea of collective self-fulfillment in the here and now. The deferred gratifications of the Long March, having led to no material paradise for workers and peasants, were transmuted into a source of continuing spiritual satisfaction; "naked morality" became an end in itself, and the revolutionary expectation of a glorious future, so long postponed, was indefinitely suspended, its place claimed once again by a heroic present. In this process the Party—whose leadership, Mao once boasted, made this revolution unprecedented as compared to earlier, failed peasant rebellions and whose group discipline Liu Shao-ch'i had hailed as superior to mere self-cultivation—would be sacrificed to the new moral struggle, pressed by an army of spontaneous, grassroots heroes in the Red Guards against the prudential ways of a lethargic Party bureaucracy.

Today this phase too has passed, having proved to be only the final paroxysm of a revolutionary nightmare. The vanguard now conducts not a protracted struggle but a rearguard action. Even a continuing or permanent revolution redefined in primarily moral terms could not easily cope with the effects on morale of a failure to realize its original material goals of industrialization and technical modernization. The celebrated "backyard furnace" might have been a dramatic symbol of native know-how, homespun practicality, and self-sufficiency, but it did not in fact fulfill the goals of modernization. As a result China has now virtually abandoned the moral struggle of the Cultural Revolution and redefined its goals in terms of a "modernization" process that stresses—mirabile dictu—"learning from facts," "pragmatism," avoiding doctrinaire attitudes, and so on. *Plus ça change, plus c'est la même chose Chinoise.*

Despite this, what has indeed changed is China's emergence from its traditional/revolutionary isolationism and, at the same time, a new openness even to the study of the Chinese past. This combination, it seems to me, promises to renew the fitful dialogue that has been going on between China and the West in modern times, and this in turn will profoundly affect all issues having to do with the future of any "ism" in China. As always, China's fate will be decided largely on its own terms, but those terms will increasingly be defined in the context of East Asia, the world, and the global future.

In conclusion, I recall the rather wry comment made to me by Sir George Sansom not long after the Chinese Communist armies had gained control of the mainland in 1949 and forced American diplomats to abandon our embassy in Nanking. Sir George observed ironically what an outcome this was for the United States, which for more than half a century had made the so-called Open Door the keystone of its China policy. As things turned out, it was only after we reconciled ourselves to this extrusion and ceased trying, like Impatient and Impulsive in Chuang Tzu's fable, to bore holes in China, that China's leaders felt free to open or close their doors as they themselves saw fit. At this point they, as masters in their own house and not as respondents to external pressure or the condign patronage of others, could find reasons of their own to open doors and even come out to meet others halfway.

5 The Post-Confucian Era

IN THE FIRST HALF OF THIS CENTURY what Westerners called the Far East was better known as East Asia to the peoples who shared, besides geographical propinquity, some common Confucian culture and use of the Chinese writing system. After World War II, however, as East Asia became partitioned by the Bamboo Curtain, it lost almost any sense of shared identity or even close contiguity. Japan and the continental rim looked to the West for protection and leadership, while the mainland was submerged in the Communist tide. "The East is Red," Mao's anthem had it, but it was only half an East.

Between Mao's global aspirations, expressed in his ideological commitment to world revolution, and China's actual isolation as well as its preoccupation with internal problems, there was little room for neighborly association with other East Asians. Mao's own assault on tradition, in fact, further loosened China's former cultural links to the rest of East Asia. Meanwhile in the West, the specter of Communist power and the sheer fact of China's size loomed large in people's minds. The "sleeping giant" had awakened, and China was now a force to be reckoned with, whether for its massive share of the world's population or for the militance of its revolutionary masses. In the shadow of this continental colossus, its smaller neighbors found little place in the sun.

Only with the passing of Mao and the downfall of the Gang of Four has this shadow passed and East Asia come into its own as something more than a string of islands and peninsulas peripheral to China. Partly this is the product of China's new trade and cultural relations with its neighbors. Even more, it reflects the balancing of China's power by the rapid rise of Japan, followed in its economic miracle by other fringe areas of East Asia, small in themselves but collectively playing an increasingly powerful role in the world economy.

This spectacular reversal did not, of course, come overnight. What suddenly invested these economic successes with a new and striking importance was China's tacit admission—and sometimes the frank acknowledgment of Mao's successors—that his revolutionary program had failed to live up to the claims made for it earlier. During the supposed Great Leap Forward, it was now revealed, China had actually fallen behind in the race for modernization—to the point where it had much to learn from both the West and East Asia.

One implication of this dramatic turn of events, for those who saw it in a larger perspective, was that true power and importance in the world were not to be gauged by numbers and size alone. Economic miracles, accompanied by wider distribution of wealth, by social, technological, and cultural advances, and above all by a great expansion of educational opportunity, have been achieved not only in Japan, confined as it is to its home islands, but in one after another of the fringe areas of East Asia; South Korea, Taiwan, Hong Kong, and Singapore. These are small, even tiny, countries compared to mainland China, and the latter's retarded modernization, compared to their rapid development, makes China look like a lumbering, if no longer slumbering, giant. Size has not proven to be the key to power and success. Indeed it might now be seen as a handicap.

Today, despite its defeat in World War II, Japan has even been declared by some the actual winner of that war. Those who remember Japan's prewar aim of building a "greater East Asia coprosperity sphere," wonder if it has not come close to accomplishing by peaceful means what it failed to win by arms. Yet in material terms Japan is a poorly endowed country with pitifully limited physical resources. This is even truer, of course, of South Korea, Taiwan, Hong Kong, and Singapore. Yet among those East Asian countries which, after the devastation of war, started to build or rebuild at midcentury, it is the losers in terms of size and natural resources that have emerged as winners in the race for economic, social, and cultural development.

As analysts, including economists and sociologists, have tried to explain this startling reversal of fortunes in the last three decades, they have increasingly turned to cultural factors as the keys. In the process, perhaps without quite realizing it, they have been redefining the real meaning of East Asia, as well as China's most significant relation to it, in cultural terms.

One reason for this belated realization is that until recently modernization had been thought of mostly in terms of rapid change, indeed, as almost invariably a revolutionary process. Few analysts stopped to think that the key to success might lie rather in deeply rooted social processes and cultural traditions. Today it would be no less fallacious to assume that such miracles could be explained solely on the basis of indigenous factors, for these successes owe much to the West and especially to postwar American aid or trade. Yet not all beneficiaries of that aid have been able to turn it to such good account as have the peoples of East Asia, and it may well be the cultural traits, skills, and disciplines brought from their past that have enabled East Asians to exploit these opportunities more fully. Further, that they have been able to do so successfully almost wherever they have emigrated, not just in their original habitat, suggests that these traits of mind and spirit are not bound to the East Asian soil.

In this respect progress is less identifiable with nation-states than with peoples or groups who have often demonstrated their capabilities in settings outside conventional national frameworks. Only in Japan has this result been identified with national development in the usual sense; in island enclaves like Hong Kong, Taiwan, Singapore, and other overseas communities, and in divided countries like Korea, this capability has been no less manifest. Even in the urban centers and university communities of the West, where substantial numbers of East Asians are making their way successfully into higher education and upper-level professions, the same capability has been demonstrated.

For my purposes here, however, I shall confine myself to East Asia and focus on what has recently been called "post-Confucian East Asia," a term expressing the idea that these successes in modernization are attributable, at least in significant part, to the continuing influence of traditional Confucian values. As I described this earlier:

> The dramatic successes of these countries in rapid modernization, by contrast to the slow pace of development elsewhere in Asia, Africa, and South America, and all the more notably in the absence of great natural resources other than their human endowment, has drawn new attention to a factor long overlooked in the common background of the peoples of East Asia: a long-shared process of intellectual and moral preparation through Neo-Confucianism. Whereas previously the Confucian influence had been seen as inimical to modernization (and it was unquestionably averse to certain aspects of westernization), the idea that the peoples of China, Japan, Korea, Taiwan, Hong Kong, and Singapore have benefited from the love of learning, commitment to education, social discipline, and personal cultivation fostered by Neo-Confucianism, can now be entertained.[1]

The concept "post-Confucian" no doubt owes much of its currency to the recent characterization of the West as "post-Christian," referring to a continuity of Christian values that have survived into the secular civilization of the modern era. Between these two cases, however, there is at least one significant difference: Christianity still has churches and other religious institutions to speak for it, as so-called "world religions" do in other lands. Confucianism, alone among the major world traditions, has today no church, no clergy, and indeed no institutional voice whatever to represent it. Saying this may only acknowledge that Confucianism does not fit the conventional definition of a "higher world religion." In that case ecumenical movements in our time are left in something of a quandary: although such movements believe that the principle of universality demands that Confucianism be represented at meetings like the World Parliament of Religions, it is difficult to find anyone certified to represent it. For us this situation has the disadvantage of leaving "post-Confucian East Asia" as a disembodied concept. Where do we look for it?

By all ordinary criteria Confucians, if any still exist, would have to be classed as stateless persons, or even placed in the "homeless" category. To some, thinking of the overly close identification of Confucianism with the old dynastic state in the late imperial age, its "stateless" condition today may represent no great loss. Homelessness, however, although not unbefitting Buddhism as a "homeless wisdom," is for Confucianism a complete contradiction. It leaves us, moreover, with a historical anomaly, at odds with the accepted view that universal religions or higher traditions are invariably carried through time by some organizational vehicle and driven by some leadership elite. Without them, how could Confucianism survive at all, much less endure into the future?

In traditional times, as we have seen, Confucianism had three main institutional strongholds: the family, the school, and the state. To these might be added local benevolent associations and regional guilds, often modeled on the family, which operated on ritual principles mostly of a Confucian kind. Chu Hsi, we recall, concerned himself especially with the family and school, but also gave special attention to local cooperative organizations on an intermediate level between family and state—organizations like neighborhood associations, community compacts, charity granaries, and local academies serving social and ritual, as well as educational, purposes.

The importance of Confucianism to the state can hardly be overemphasized, for it is probably to the Confucian ethos and Confucian scholarship that the Chinese dynastic state owed much of its stability and bureaucratic continuity, as compared to the relative instability of dynastic regimes in India. Yet the reverse was not equally true; Confucianism was less dependent on the state for survival than the state on it. Even though affected by the rise and fall of dynasties, Confucianism found ways to survive.

One such way was through the schools. In the modern period, even though the established forms of higher Confucian culture suffered from the destruction of the traditional social and political elites, the respect for learning that had been inculcated by the spread of Neo-Confucian education remained a powerful stimulus to the acquisition of new learning. Even with the abrupt change in the *content* of instruction, this deep-seated love of learning in peoples long imbued with Confucian values proved to be a source of continuing energy and adaptability, withstanding, in China itself, even the wholesale assault on learning of the Cultural Revolution.

Not long ago, amid the prevailing denigration of Confucianism, there was widespread doubt that it could have contributed anything to modernization. Assertions to the contrary fell on deaf ears. In the last two decades, however, there has been a dramatic reversal of this attitude. While people have spoken of economic "miracles," in fact the stunning advances in modernization—social and cultural as well as commercial and industrial—were strongly abetted by the rapid rise and spread of education, especially of higher education. Lest this be dismissed perhaps as no more than state-driven mass production—the product of an educational forced march pressed by authoritarian regimes—it should be noted that the most striking feature of this learning explosion has been a spectacular growth of private higher education in Japan, Korea, and Taiwan. Spontaneous popular demand has far outgrown the capacities of state-sponsored institutions. And increasingly this demand for more and more education has been attributed, by those close to the scene, to Confucian influence. As a professor of education at Seoul National University explained this "zeal for education," or "educational fever" (in his words), it actually had "deep roots in Korean culture," prime among them the fact that Koreans had "long been influenced by a Confucian culture which admired letters and respected learning."[2] A similar explanation has often been given for similar phenomenal growth elsewhere in the islands of East Asia.

Once one recognizes the persistence of traditional attitudes in the midst of the modernization process, the question naturally arises whether other traditions than the Confucian played a part. I have already suggested that Shinto, bushidō, "national learning," and the survival of long-standing feudal traditions had a role in Japan's rapid transformation. The influence of Buddhism too must be considered. Here, however, I think one must make some distinction between the influence of these religions on the spiritual and moral formation of East Asian peoples, which was considerable in some cases, and their role specifically in matters of learning and education. Without denying the spiritual and moral influence of Buddhism, or in Japan, of Shinto, I think one has to question whether they contributed intellectually to the actual shaping of education. With the rise and spread of Neo-

Confucianism (from the thirteenth century in China, the fourteenth in Korea, and the seventeenth in Japan), it became the dominant force in education. In fact secular education (as distinct from training for the religious life) was largely a Neo-Confucian product, and even when Buddhists engaged in it, whether for lay or clerical purposes, the content of such instruction was generally Confucian. The reason for this is not that the Buddhists had forever "left the world" and turned their backs on such secular concerns, but rather that upon returning to the world with the higher religious wisdom, they readily adapted it to, and in effect largely accepted, the prevailing culture and pattern of lay life. Thus their reaffirmation of concern for the world often took the form of showing how they accepted and promoted Confucian norms of conduct and learning, as they did to varying degrees in those situations where lay instruction was actually carried out by Buddhists in local temples and monasteries. In the more recent premodern period this instruction was mostly based on Neo-Confucian texts.

Still, at this point one must take into account two limitations of Neo-Confucian education itself. In Chapter 4 I emphasized the failure to achieve Chu Hsi's aim of providing universal schooling directed toward the general uplifting of human society. One effect of this was that for the most part schooling in China served the needs of the state bureaucracy rather than those of society at large. In turn, the leadership elite in each society tried to remedy this lack by developing its own schools and academies through local initiative. This effort appears to have been more successful in Korea and Japan than in China, but in any case it suffered from the inherent limitation that education mostly served an upper class. In China, especially, amid the intense struggle for survival among any such voluntary and fiduciary institutions, the local or "private" academies experienced great attrition from generation to generation. Even the few academies that managed to maintain some tenuous continuity over the years had to be repeatedly revived and rebuilt. More often than not it was local families, with the help of individual scholar-teachers conscious of their role as bearers of the cultural tradition, who took the lead in this.[3]

This leaves us, not surprisingly, with the family as probably the most durable home base for Confucianism, which served as a family ethic and also stimulated the family's intense demand and drive for education. What is more, this appears to have been true of the "family" or "clan" across the board in East Asia, regardless of differences in political and social organization.

Before the advance of the West, with its revolutionary impact on traditional societies, Confucianism, especially as it had become deeply involved in the social order during the Neo-Confucian phase, tended to be implicated in and greatly discredited by the collapse of traditional institutions. Unable to maintain itself in school and state, it also suffered a loss of influence in the family. Much that was identified (sometimes mistakenly) with the Neo-Confucian family system was severely criticized in the liberal and liberation movements of the early twentieth century, and many old customs were abandoned. Notwithstanding this, the family system, or at least some vital core of it, has shown a surprising resilience to the rapid changes and pressures of modern life, as if it still could provide, in intensely demanding and trying times, a moral, emotional, and corporal support that nothing else has.

This resilience is not surprising in view of past history; rather it confirms the experience of previous ages. During the formative stage of East Asian development, as we saw earlier, the relationship of Confucianism to the state was quite problematical and remained ambiguous even after Confucianism had become a kind of state teaching, since doctrine often stood in contrast to state practice. Moreover, the very instability of dynastic regimes left Confucianism in an insecure position. It endured through such vicissitudes to become the embodiment of traditional social norms in China as the so-called "normative teaching" (*ming-chiao*) more through its solid footing in family and clan life than through its state connections or schools.

Even during the second period of Buddhist religious dominance this remained true, since the chief resistance to Buddhism arose from the family on the ground that Buddhism was, allegedly, incompatible with Confucian family values; Buddhism's denial of the charge, disavowing any such intention, even went so far as to profess wholehearted commitment to Confucian family values—though this was a pledge to be redeemed in its own spiritual coin: religious merit applied to the salvation of souls. Finally, in the third stage, the family ethic was powerfully reinforced as the core of Neo-Confucian teaching and practice, and Chu Hsi's *Family Ritual* (*Chia li*), along with the *Elementary Learning* (*Hsiao hsüeh*) became basic social manuals in much of East Asia. Hence, long entrenched in this fashion, Confucianism in modern times was able, through its hold on the family, to survive the demise of traditional ruling regimes throughout East Asia and the wholesale replacement of Confucian schools by Western-style learning.

In the discussion of post-Confucian East Asia, however, the values that have been most emphasized are self-discipline, group loyalty, frugality, self-denial, and obedience to authority—in short, the values of the work ethic and those presumed congenial to authoritarian political structures. Much of the discussion relative to Japan has focused on the work ethic as it developed in the Tokugawa period, from the seventeenth to the nineteenth century, sometimes described as "bourgeois Confucianism." Often this is cited as an important background factor in Japan's business success. Yet this ethic has its counterparts in China and Korea as well, which compels us to reckon with two of its basic characteristics.

First, historically many of these values have been shared among different classes, especially peasants, and are by no means limited to merchants or townspeople (the "bourgeoisie"). Second, in the most general terms, these values may perhaps best be understood as the basic values of a Confucian family ethic, which, in a sense, cuts across classes, operates in more than one economic sphere, and has proven adaptable, as I indicated before, to quite different social and political systems.

When one speaks of its adaptability to different systems, however, one must beware of the common assertion that Confucianism engendered an attitude of passive acquiescence in, if not servile obedience to, all forms of established authority. No doubt some respect for authority is involved, since a work ethic presupposes the maintenance of an ordered environment, stable and secure enough for its practitioners to thrive in. But as Sun Yat-sen discovered, when he tried to operate politically at the interface of the traditional Chinese social system with the political and economic processes of the modern West, it was not easy to appropriate traditional loyalties and disciplines to the needs of a modern state and party. At this juncture Sun complained about the excessive "individualism" and primary family loyalty of the Chinese—and for good reason, since these loyalties were not at the disposal of just any authoritarian state or leader. They grew out of a Neo-Confucian order of priorities based on the self and family, which took into account human motivations for work or service—not just a passive obedience to superior authority but a sense of positive identification with a shared enterprise, yielding mutual benefits.

If we understand this sense as a deep-seated need in East Asian societies and a common assumption among the major ethicoreligious traditions, we can appreciate the positive energies that often flow from traditional disciplines, and not just their negative features. Recently the *New York Times* thought it newsworthy to report on the workings of the so-called *gyeh* organizations among immigrant Koreans in the New York area. The *gyeh* was decribed as a cooperative group that "carried forward a centuries-old custom of mutual trust that has made it possible for hundreds of Korean immigrants to open businesses in the city, businesses that have revitalized neighborhoods and increased the impact this particular ethnic group has had on New York."[4] Referred to as a kind of credit union, the *gyeh* also has benevolent and social functions. A member was quoted as saying that the families come together "not just for the money," but "to see our friends and exchange information." Everything depends, he said, on "mutual trust" and on a "code of honor that is part of the Koreans' heritage."

Students of Korean history and society will recognize that the *gyeh* does indeed have a long tradition behind it—a tradition that proved highly receptive to Chu Hsi's recommendations concerning the "community compacts" and the social ethic accompanying them, stressing individual responsibility, mutual respect, and neighborly cooperation.[5] It may be too soon to judge how well these attitudes and associations will survive the brutalization of American city life, but at least this example helps us to see that there is more to the traditional ethic than just a Mafia-like mentality of submission to bosses wielding "patriarchal authority" (an expression often resorted to by writers on the post-Confucian ethic).

A related question has to do with the adaptability of the Confucian ethic to modern capitalism. Here two issues generally arise. The first concerns a presumed "Confucian" amenability to the paternalism often found in East Asian industrial enterprises—a factor heralded by some as conducive to efficiency and productivity and decried by others as lending itself to exploitation of the worker. Both ends may be served by an ethic stressing hard work, frugality, and self-sacrifice. No doubt in many cases severe exploitation occurs. But often too an element of reciprocity is involved, even though it is not readily detected or quantified, and a sense of personal identification with the enterprise and its leadership is fostered. There are trade-offs of a humane or benevolent character, such as security against layoffs, and these trade-offs render working conditions at least tolerable, if they do not actually make for a lasting and meaningful association. Given these two possibilities, what makes an assessment in Confucian terms difficult to come by is precisely the lack today of anyone both informed and qualified to speak for Confucianism. Indeed, whether any such spokesperson will appear remains a question. In the past, however, Confucianism's strong point has been its concern for human relations; whether it will have anything significant to say about labor relations could prove to be one test of its relevance to the modern world.

The second issue has to do with capitalism and the profit motive. Is the Confucian concept of virtue compatible with either? Here Mencius is often cited as denigrating profit (*li*) and contrasting to it what is right and proper (*i*). According to this high standard of rectitude, the pursuit of virtue precludes the seeking of personal gain or utility, and there is no room for utilitarianism or the profit motive in Confucianism. The issue remains a central one in later Confucian thought, where it tends to become compounded with the issue of what is in one's private or selfish interest (*ssu*) and what is in the common or public interest (*kung*). It also becomes confused, in later dynastic settings, with attitudes originally promoted by the Legalist school of thought, such as a hostility to commerce and a desire to restrict the activities of the merchant class. If one examines early Confucian writings, one does not find in them the same hostility. For Mencius and Hsun Tzu commerce is not an evil, and nothing suggests that merchants are to be subjected to the disabilities Legalists would impose on them. Those disabilities arise more from the merchants' conflict with the bureaucratic class and from the dynastic state's having a greater interest in economic control than in economic development, rather than from any inherent Confucian antipathy to commerce.

For Confucians the applicable criteria would be the subordination of the profit motive, as serving individual self-interest, to the greater good of the commonalty. For the family this has meant sharing profits and spreading benefits among relatives, an attitude that worked against capital formation and aggressive entrepreneurship in traditional China but did not totally rule them out. In government, for the Confucians, it meant that the mandarinate should not engage in profit-seeking at the expense of the people or use its public role to private advantage. In practice this led often to a kind of collusive profit-sharing collaboration between merchants and officials, but also to a stalemate in which neither the middle class nor the government, so restricted, took up the active promotion of economic enterprise.

Some observers have concluded from these facts that Confucianism, with its emphasis on the commonalty rather than the individual, was more compatible in the modern world with socialism and communism than with capitalism. To me this is at most a half truth and misses the real point. Since the model for the commonalty was the family, the essential criterion has been whether economic activity, including capitalist activity, served the long-term interests and values of the family or, by extension, the state as a whole.

If this criterion was lost sight of by those who leapt to the conclusion that Confucian values were more conducive to state socialism than to capitalism, it also tends to be forgotten by those who think that the so-called "capitalist" tendencies of the post-Mao regime will necessarily produce a Western-style capitalism. In my opinion recent reforms are more likely to foster relatively small-scale, family-style capitalism than the large-scale corporate enterprise of the West, though it has been shown that in late Ch'ing China, Taiwan, and Japan, entrepreneurial functions on a fairly large scale could be carried on through extended-family or multifamily enterprises. In mainland China under Communist rule the prognosis is for a configuration not very different from the traditional one— much small-scale, family-style entrepreneurship on the local level and a continued role for the state in the management or control of larger economic enterprises. If I am right in this conjecture, the new Chinese "capitalism" will also conform to tradition in that it will be less individualistic than the typical Western variety, or at least the role of the individual will be conceived more within the context of family life and values. This point, I think, is often overlooked by contemporary observers who hail the new trends in the People's Republic as "capitalistic" without looking at them in the perspective of Chinese history and society.

The other main point to be dealt with in relation to post-Confucian East Asia is the assumption that Confucian social discipline necessarily lends itself to authoritarian political structures. Strong leadership may indeed, in certain situations, produce the political stability needed for economic development, and one cannot deny that this has tended to be the case in much of East Asia. But strong leadership alone will not suffice, as witness the failure of the "great leader and helmsman," Mao Tse-tung.

To the extent that the persistence of Confucian values might be looked upon as contributing to social and political stability, we should remember that side of the Confucian tradition that has always dwelt on the nature of true leadership, as expressed in the concept of the *chün-tzu*, or noble man. Here the emphasis has been on the leadership's responsibility to and for the people and on the need for consultative processes to assure that leaders are properly informed and advised. I have discussed this in *The Liberal Tradition in China*, but one may certainly question whether this can be considered a live tradition—whether, after so many revolutionary upheavals, it is grounded in any social reality such as the continuity of family life still seems to represent.

The Confucians never organized a political party, led a revolution, or seized power. Whether Confucianism has ever been a political ideology or not, I do not see its becoming one in present circumstances. It may well regain some place in the educational process, but how this would translate into political action depends largely on the existence and extent of freedom of communication and association.

Yet this situation would not be entirely new for the Confucians, least of all for Confucius himself and for those who understood him well. Remember the opening lines of the *Analects,* quoted in Chapter 1: "To be unrecognized [politically speaking] and yet remain unembittered, is that not to be [truly] a 'noble man'?" In Confucius' eyes, one need not hold public office in order to render a public service or fulfill one's social responsibility.[6] Confucius' account of his own life expressed a sense of personal fulfillment despite his lack of political success.[7] Chu Hsi and Wang Yang-ming too were among the later Confucians who survived political failure and left on their followers an impression of serene nobility of soul. Such men as these could live, even out of office, without a frightful sense of anxiety, disappointment, or final predicament. Nor would it be a criterion of the success or failure of Confucianism today whether it was able to constitute a new "Confucian" mandarinate.

In mainland China itself we may well be facing a historically irreversible situation with respect to basic institutional structures, not unlike the Ch'in-Han situation, wherein the best that could realistically be expected was a slow, long-term modification of new state structures through the humanizing of their administration. Again education would be the key, along with freer communication, to enable some form of electoral process gradually to become incorporated into the basic pattern. If we define the only prospect of improvement in contemporary terms as "socialism with a human face," that "socialism" is already mixed and the "human face" may well partake increasingly of a Confucian humanism that is open to the world of others' political experience, perhaps especially that of other East Asians. If this change does not develop, China will suffer from a despotism far worse than anything seen in traditional dynasties, because it will be far more totalitarian and technocratic in its controls.

In the past, leading Neo-Confucians questioned the legitimacy of dynastic rule or the validity of dynastic law, though most Confucians who agreed to take office reconciled themselves to both of these as inescapable facts of life. The same now is happening with Communist rule, which one hears spoken of as a new dynasty or a new feudalism. Most essentially the similarity lies in the unquestioned character of rule by the regnant party, as sacrosanct as dynastic rule or dynastic law ever was. Despite failures and catastrophes far more serious than anything that would bring down a government in a parliamentary or electoral system, the continued rule of the Communist party remains beyond question. However people may talk about the diversity of Communist systems, in this respect the systems are one: no matter how great the government's failure, the party does not accept responsibility for it, with the usual implications of resigning and allowing another party to take responsibility. Instead a former leader is made the scapegoat—in Russia, Stalin, or Beria; in Poland, Gomulka or Giereck; in China, Mao or Lin Piao; in Cambodia, Pol Pot—while the party, like the imperial dynasty but with an even more absolute claim to sovereignty, retains a dictatorial power not subject even to the mandate of Heaven.

The Confucians, it is true, always felt it important to have a well-defined structure of authority, for this was a way of making explicit the differentiated responsibilities individuals bore to one another, or dynasties bore to Heaven and its people. Yet most observers familiar with the workings of the

Chinese family system—or with other East Asian family systems influenced to some degree by Confucianism—would, I think, recognize that their actual workings have been marked by a large measure of family consultation and cooperation and not simply by the imposition of autocratic authority. I would not venture to say how this *modus operandi* can best be adapted to the conditions of modern political life, but a true awareness and appreciation of this tradition of consultation would at least warn against any easy assumption that Confucianism necessarily lends itself to dictatorial rule. It depends, for the Confucian, on how one conceives of authority and how well, in the end, the exercise of that authority through consultative processes serves to enhance human dignity and the viability of the human enterprise. This latter, in turn, must include in its vision the fate of the earth and all that Confucians traditionally embraced in the concept of a "humaneness forming one body with Heaven, Earth and all things."

As long as China remained predominantly an agricultural civilization, the intimate association of humankind with Heaven, Earth, and all things was, in some degree, a daily experience for all. Now that it has entered the industrial and technological age, not only is that close association being weakened, but the earlier holistic vision has become overcast by the specters of pollution and man-made environmental catastrophes.

Thus to me it is evident that, just as no one people can deal with these new threats alone, neither can one expect to pursue the earlier vision by drawing on the resources of Confucianism alone. For China, as for the rest of East Asia, dealing with new circumstances will involve a process of growth, as it has in the past for Confucianism—a reaching out to share in the experience of other peoples, religions, and ethical traditions, yet now through an expanded dialogue that goes beyond anything seen before.

6 East Asia and the West: Catching Up with Each Other

NO REAL DIALOGUE CAN TAKE PLACE between East Asia and the West unless both parties are equally and deeply involved, but for all the West's desire to understand East Asians, so far its effort has not been equal to theirs. This may be an odd time to raise the issue, since interest in East Asia had never been higher in the West than it is now, and the achievements, in both economic and cultural terms, of the East Asian peoples are more respected today than ever before. Nevertheless if I return now to the question posed at the beginning of Chapter 4—whether the West might need to catch up with East Asia—I do so not only in the obvious sense that East Asia has now overtaken us in several economic areas and that America must become more efficient or proficient if it is to compete. I mean rather that we have not yet grasped the deeper meaning of our encounter with East Asia or adjusted to the new reality of the Old World discovered there.

We have long since passed the last frontier of outward, westward expansion (the bounds of the original New World), but we have not realized that our new frontier must be conceived in terms other than further penetration into others' space. Rather we must learn to live with both ourselves and others as East Asians have been doing for centuries—by a deeper, more intensive cultivation of our limited space, which

is to say much more of an "inner space" than an open frontier or "outer space." Whatever mission we still have to perform in East or West—whether it be religious, educational,
political, legal, or any other cause one feels called on to take
up—must adjust to this reality. Yet the West, facing this new
fact of life, the end of the road for its long outward journey,
has been as unprepared to accept it as the East Asians were to
come out of their world into ours.

To illustrate the point, let me cite the case, not too long
ago, of a columnist for the *Wall Street Journal* who adduced
the negative example of China in arguing for the aggressive
exploration and development of space. In an article entitled
"Mandarin Mondale and the U.S. Future in Space," the
writer set up Walter Mondale as a modern mandarin, liken-
ing him to the Confucian Chinese of the fifteenth and sixteenth centuries who put a stop to the voyages of Cheng Ho
and Chinese maritime exploration, just as, according to this
interpretation, Mondale would have put a stop to U.S. space
exploration.[1] The author quoted such authorities as the "au-
thor-physicist" Arthur Kantrowitz, Joseph Needham, and
Jung-pang Lo on behalf of his view that, at this crucial turning point in history, the Chinese went into "a general decline," a "depression of the spirit" that overtook the Chinese
"desire to learn" and inhibited "the temper and spirit of the
Chinese people." This reversal and decline he attributed, not
altogether incorrectly, to the influence of "the champions of
Chinese standpattism: the Confucian bureaucrats."

> For political and cultural reasons, these Mandarin bu-
> reaucrats hated the "outward bound" policy of the trea-
> sure ships and their admirals. In Mr. Needham's words:
> "The Grand Fleet of Treasure Ships swallowed up funds
> which, in the view of all right-thinking bureaucrats,
> would be much better spent on water-conservancy proj-
> ects for the farmers' needs, or in agrarian financing,

'ever-normal granaries' and the like." Under their influence, Chinese science ossified and, even worse, became divorced from technology. And this, the ongoing
partnership of science and nuts-and-bolts technology,
was what gave Western civilization the edge it has kept
to the present.[2]

We need not concern ourselves with the political conclusions
drawn here, but observe rather the manner in which the
writer dismisses the moral position of the so-called Confucian bureaucrats:

> To the argument that we can no longer afford large-scale
> exploration of space, I would respond that hindsight
> makes it clear that the destruction of the Ming navy was
> the real extravagance . . . As in Ming China, there are
> those who have gained center stage by its suppression.
> The suppressors in both cases claim moral superiority
> and have too often been able to conceal the magnificent
> role of creative technology in liberating and elevating
> mankind.
> Three hundred years after Cheng Ho and the great
> treasure fleets, a Chinese ruler did build a rather impres-
> sive ship: a full-size barge made of solid marble. If our
> modern Mandarins get to run things, we might have a
> marble space shuttle down in Houston—you know,
> something to really impress the Russians and Japanese.[3]

The article would be of only passing moment were it not
that it invoked one of the most indelible images of dynastic
China—the marble pleasure boat in the Summer Palace near
Peking—which virtually all visitors to China are shown as
typifying the misplaced values of the traditional order. What
I wish to single out is the easy assumption that the Confucian
position too can be disposed of simply by pointing to the

same bizarre example. It is an assumption rendered plausible by the view, dominating the whole article, that the Confucians clearly went wrong, that they failed to keep up with "the spirit of expansion and enterprise" and were so addicted to the notion of their moral superiority that they could see no use whatever for science and technology—certainly a vast oversimplification.

I do not wish to argue here either for or against Mondale's supposedly "liberal" position on "star wars" (a view which, in a more fundamental sense, might be thought conservative as opposed to expansive). My concern is rather with the question of who is being short-sighted and parochial here and who is being realistic. Realism, it seems to me, would require us to question seriously a policy of indefinite expansionism and exploitation of the earth's human and physical resources, and not just dismiss this thought as already discredited by Chinese history. What is presented here as a more open and expansive view of the human enterprise may actually be a narrow, parochial one.

Lest my own view be misunderstood as calling for a limiting of intellectual or scientific horizons, the need I see is rather for a better sense of where we stand, of the home base from which we start in reaching out to take on global challenges. Along with an awareness of new possibilities for learning and growth, and prerequisite to exploring them, we must have a sense of direction, of context, of due process, and of deliberate speed in our use of present resources, both human and physical.

This is no more a conservative view than it is a liberal one, since being conservative as to means does not preclude liberal ends and may indeed be the only practical way to advance them. Nor does it ignore the possibility that real and present dangers to basic human values may even, in some circumstances, call for prophetic vision or radical action. Such options would exist even in circumstances recognized as severely limiting, just as within the limited horizons of the Confucian world there were both liberal and conservative tendencies, both scholarly and prophetic voices. It does, however, mean accepting the idea that freedom may be found elsewhere than in recourse to a great liberality of means, the exploitation of material resources, or the conquest of space. The discovery of true freedom and creativity comes only in limiting contexts, when we are compelled to draw more deeply on inner resources of the human spirit. Indeed, do we not already witness such liberating possibilities in the current popularity of the traditional arts of Asia, whether martial, cultural, or contemplative, the challenge of which is precisely to self-mastery and deeper spiritual creativity in clearly defined contexts?

Similarly in the social order, a more truly open and cosmopolitan—or I should say planetary—outlook might require a more Confucian view of our primary responsibilities. It would have to consider whether our most deep-seated problem in a world of rapid and almost compulsive change may not be the lack of any parochial loyalties in the sense of a responsibility to any given human or earth community. What we need is not new worlds to conquer, star wars and all that, but a new parochialism of the earth or planet. This should start, as the Confucians did, with self-reflection and self-restraint. Conscious of the interrelatedness of all things, and of one's own place in an interdependent world, this view should develop a sense of equal responsibility for oneself and others and of reciprocal support for a life-sustaining environment. It would address the question of what we will *not* do, what choices we will voluntarily forgo, what limitations we will accept out of concern for the welfare of our earth, our fellow man, and the generations to come who will otherwise suffer for our sins of earth pollution, resource exhaustion, genetic disorders, and so on.

In view of our past history, it is natural enough for us to

project a future of unlimited expansion into outer space—the "conquest of space" as contemporary conquistadors put it, now that they have given up singing "Onward Christian Soldiers." But as we contemplate such an endless, aimless adventure, we should pause to consider whether it does not, after all, manifest a compulsive drive to control everything but ourselves, lest we stop long enough to discover a great emptiness within. If it is not hubris that propels us to this incredible ambition to dominate, it may well be the lack of any genuine self-satisfaction. Not being at peace with ourselves and failing to come to terms with the world ("taking responsibility for oneself," as the Confucians put it, and for all those actions that affect the lives of other beings), we are driven by an ever-deepening addiction, the vain idea that success and satisfaction must be out there somewhere just over the horizon. Just so, the astronomer Carl Sagan, though at opposite poles politically from the defender of star wars, insists that we set as our national goal the placing of man on Mars, lest we lose the momentum for great achievements—as if no task, no pressing human need closer to our home on earth, could compel our attention or be worthy of our noblest aspirations.

We have lived so long on the "high" of rising expectations, on the "speed" of constantly accelerated, fossil-fueled locomotion, on the stimulation of our jaded appetites by advertising that can sell us only what is souped up as "exciting," "shocking," "fantastic," or "out of this world," that it seems normal and natural for a whole society to live on credit cards and wildly unbalanced national budgets, throwing more and more dollars at problems that do not yield to quantitative solutions, even at the risk of runaway inflation and eventual catastrophic collapse.

Some indeed cry out, "Stop the world, I want to get off"; others think of sitting it out in a Zen monastery or in transcendental meditation (recognizing to this extent at least that the East has antidotes, if not anodynes, for such disorders of the spirit). But many more are like the character Monkey in the Chinese novel *Journey to the West*. As the story goes, the Monkey King had ambitions to seize the throne of the Jade Emperor, but the Lord Buddha stopped him. To settle the matter they agreed on a wager. If Monkey could jump off the palm of the Buddha's hand, he would have the throne. " 'This Buddha,' Monkey thought to himself, 'is a perfect fool. I can jump a hundred and eight thousand leagues, while his palm cannot be as much as eight inches across. How could I fail to jump clear of it.' "[4]

Monkey leapt with all his might, whizzing by so fast that the Buddha, watching him with the eye of wisdom, saw a mere whirligig shoot along. Then:

> Monkey came at last to five pink pillars, sticking up into the air. "This is the end of the World," said Monkey to himself. "All I have got to do is to go back to Buddha and claim my forfeit. The Throne is mine." "Wait a minute," he said presently, "I'd better just leave a record of some kind, in case I have trouble with Buddha." He plucked a hair and blew on it with magic breath, crying "Change!" It changed at once into a writing brush charged with heavy ink, and at the base of the central pillar he wrote, "The Great Sage Equal to Heaven reached this place." Then to mark his disrespect, he relieved nature at the bottom of the first pillar, and somersaulted back to where he had come from. Standing on Buddha's palm, he said, "Well, I've gone and come back. You can go and tell the Jade Emperor to hand over the Palaces of Heaven." "You stinking ape," said Buddha, "you've been on the palm of my hand all the time." "You're quite mistaken," said Monkey. "I got to the end of the World, where I saw five flesh-coloured pillars sticking up into the sky. I wrote something on one of them. I'll take you there and show you, if you like." "No

need for that," said Buddha. "Just look down." Monkey peered down with his fiery, steely eyes, and there at the base of the middle finger of Buddha's hand he saw written the words "The Great Sage Equal to Heaven reached this place," and from the fork between the thumb and first finger came a smell of monkey's urine. It took him some time to get over his astonishment. At last he said, "Impossible, impossible! I wrote that on the pillar sticking up into the sky. How did it get on to Buddha's finger? He's practising some magic upon me. Let me go back and look." Dear Monkey! He crouched, and was just making ready to spring again, when Buddha turned his head, and pushed Monkey out at the western gate of Heaven.[5]

In the end Monkey had to give up his world-conquering ambitions and submit to the restraint and direction of the humble, plodding pilgrim Tripitaka in order to achieve enlightenment. I shall forgo the temptation to allegorize here. I do not mean to equate Monkey with the bumptious West or Tripitaka with the wisdom of the East, as if they were antithetical rather than complementary (as the original *Journey* had it). Nor do I wish to moralize about space conquerors carrying their stinking pollution to the ends of the universe (perhaps the more insidious, because less detectable, when it does *not* stink!). Rather I confine myself to one observation: that no matter how far we hurtle through space, even if there is no one to "throw us out of Heaven," we shall still have to return to Mother Earth and face the unresolved, inescapable problems left behind there.

We may have to look at the situation with the Confucian eyes of Hsia Yüan-chi, the Ming Yung-lo Emperor's fiscal genius, who provided the logistic support for Cheng Ho's voyages. Hsia was open to the thought that these voyages might explore terra incognita and expand China's economic horizons; his was not a closed mind. Yet in the end, weighing the great human costs against the ephemeral returns, he opposed their continuance and carried on his protest to the point of incurring imprisonment, risking indeed even death. How much less would he have acquiesced in the empress dowager's marble boat!

The Confucians faced many of these questions as early as the eleventh century, though not on quite the scale or with the same complexity as we must today. Sung civilization, as we have seen, had reached the point where new technologies could be suitably applied to solving its urgent problems (demographically speaking, be it noted, of modern proportions). Hu Yüan believed that in education the humane values of the Confucian classics were needed to guide the application of the more concentrated political power and sophisticated technology available in his day. Thus his curriculum included classical studies for basic principles ("substance") and technical studies for practical application ("function"). Chu Hsi, for his part, developed the "substance" aspect further in his philosophy of human nature and the moral mind, but most especially in a cosmology that saw man's moral consciousness as coaxial with the life-giving and life-sustaining powers of Heaven-and-Earth.

If as a philosopher Chu Hsi thought it essential to ground his philosophy of human nature in such a cosmology and did not simply assume that man was the measure of all things, as a teacher he thought it no less vital for education to be centered on the self and the home. Working out from that center, as one disciplined and developed one's powers, one could take on ever-expanding tasks and opportunities for humane endeavor.

In this context it is understandable that nineteenth-century Neo-Confucians, though impressed by the power and technology of the West and compelled to come to terms with it, still harbored grave, unresolved doubts. How could one pursue the seemingly unlimited development of power and technology without asking what commensurate conception of the moral center would hold these centrifugal forces within bounds or direct them to the humane ends traditionally summed up in "a humanity forming one body with Heaven-and-Earth and all things" (that is, feeling for all things as if they were your own flesh and blood)?

Some East Asians are still looking for an answer, while others have long since ceased even to ask the question. Many simply follow the dominant trend in the West, where increasingly it appears that, in dealing with severe social problems, self-restraint and moral guidance are no longer considered acceptable options. Rather the West's solution often seems to be in impersonal, mechanical means—material inducements, legal sanctions, penal institutions—that have already proven ineffective. The expenditure of more and more money, with less and less attention to the deeper problems of the human spirit, leads only to bankruptcy.

There is of course another side to the "West," which stands in significant contrast to this dominant trend and offers some hope of reversing it. This may best be identified with the environmental movement, which, when it has not lent itself to ulterior, ideological ends, has shown remarkable dynamism as a grassroots effort cutting across the political spectrum. Although it is still far from achieving its larger objectives, what it has already accomplished in a few short decades to reduce air, water, and earth pollution (especially smoking) is a major triumph. That these gains have been made largely by voluntary educational efforts, with a minimum of legal coercion (while more tightly controlled and planned societies have done little), is a great credit to the popular initiative and leadership of the movement in Western democracies.

Ironically, since Oriental philosophies in the form of "nature mysticism" are often seen as a source of inspiration for such movements, we have the apparent paradox of the West, with its cultural and political pluralism, taking over certain aspects of the East Asian tradition, while modern East Asia, industrialized and commercialized almost with a vengeance, lags behind in the struggle to control pollution. In this respect, then, the meeting and mixing of East and West have already progressed to the point where modern East Asia may need to catch up with some of its best traditions, as exemplified by the West.

What may seem even more paradoxical is the official alarm expressed in the People's Republic of China, which is formally committed to a materialist philosophy and is now admittedly pursuing a "pragmatic" policy, over the alleged danger of moral degeneration and spiritual contamination from the West. Some observers would discount this as more truly designed to curb people's pent-up desires for the good things of life and to justify the continued repression of human rights and freedom of thought. One cannot rule this out, certainly, as a subconscious motive. Having defaulted on many of the original promises of the revolution, made to justify the seizure of power by a party dictatorship, its leaders now reach out for new justifications that may appeal to popular prejudices, including an old-fashioned fundamentalist morality. Thus they use the defense of traditional virtue as a cloak for the preservation of their own authority.

Yet it would be a mistake to assume that no more is at issue, or at work, than this. Similar doubts and fears have been expressed over the years, in most East Asian countries, by spokesmen of both right and left, by elements of the establishment and of the opposition to it, by radicals of the Cultural Revolution as well as by more moderate, secular socialists like Lee Kwan-yu of Singapore who broods, as the liberal Nehru once did also, over the moral corruption that "Westernization" seems to bring in its train.

Nor do these apprehensions represent only Asia's stubborn rearguard action against the West. Similar fears beset the

West itself. As one particularly apt expression of this sentiment, let me quote in conclusion from an essay written by Lionel Trilling just before his death, in which he tried to diagnose as an American problem what we recognize as a worldwide malaise:

If we consider the roadblocks in the path of a reestablishment of traditional humanistic education, surely none is so effectually obstructing as the tendency of our culture to regard the mere energy of impulse as being in every mental and moral way equivalent and even superior to defined intention. We may remark, as exemplary of this tendency, the fate of an idea that once was salient in Western culture: the idea of "making a life," by which was meant conceiving human existence, one's own or another's, as if it were a work of art upon which one might pass judgment, assessing it by established criteria.

This desire to fashion, to shape, a self and a life has all but gone from a contemporary culture whose emphasis, paradoxically enough, is so much on self . . . Such limitation, once acceptable, now goes against the cultural grain—it is almost as if the fluidity of the contemporary world demands an analogous limitlessness in our personal perspective. Any doctrine, that of the family, religion, the school, that does not sustain this increasingly felt need for a multiplicity of options and instead offers an ideal of a shaped self, a formed life, has the sign on it of a retrograde and depriving authority, which, it is felt, must be resisted.

For anyone concerned with contemporary education at whatever level, the assimilation that contemporary culture has made between social idealism, even political liberalism, and personal fluidity—a self without the old confinements—is as momentous as it is recalcitrant to correction. Among the factors in the contemporary world which militate against the formulation of an educational ideal related to the humanistic traditions of the past, this seems to me to be the most decisive.[6]

If Trilling seems to agonize here over aberrations of the counterculture in the sixties, with its drive toward liberation from all constraints of tradition, there may well have been, in the inchoate cross-currents of that age, many whose radicalism was less political than moral and spiritual, and who sought desperately to shape a life, to define a self, precisely at a time when the permissiveness of their elders offered them little real challenge or reliable guidance. The frequent incantation in those days, "Not to decide is to decide," may often have been abused in the absence of persuasive evidence on which to base a decision, but it did not reflect a sense of the "limitlessness of personal perspective," in Trilling's phrase.

In such circumstances tradition would appear to have failed, and young persons, in a generation unmoored to any meaningful past, would be apt to ignore the claims of history. On this point, a decade later in 1986, one of Trilling's successors as Jefferson Lecturer, Leszek Kolakowski, had this to say about the nature of historical self-understanding:

> Educated (and even un-educated) people in pre-industrial societies, whose historical learning was very meager, were perhaps more historical—in the sense I mean here—than we are. The historical tradition in which they lived was woven of myths, legends and orally-transmitted stories of which the material accuracy was more often than not dubious. Still it was good enough to give them the feeling of life within a continuous religious, national or tribal community, to provide them with the kind of identity that made life ordered (or "meaningful"). In this sense it was a living thing, and it

taught people why, and for what they were responsible, as well as how this responsibility was to be practically taken up . . . But whoever is interested in, and worrying about, the spiritual fragility of young people cannot deny that the erosion of a historically-defined sense of "belonging" plays havoc with their lives, and threatens their ability to withstand possible trials of the future.[7]

Kolakowski, speaking also to the question of personal rights in the modern world, says that they are defensible "only on the assumption that there is a realm of personal reality that is definable in moral, not biological terms. They have to be vindicated on moral grounds, much as their implementation depends on political conditions."[8]

Confucians would have resisted the dichotomy of moral/biological here, but what both Trilling and Kolakowski saw as key to the crisis in modern education—a dialogue with the past—was already central to the teaching of Confucius in the sixth century B.C. and remained so in the dialogue conducted by the Confucians down through the ages, in converse with other traditions and cultures. The Japanese particularly set that dialogue in a multicultural context and kept it open to new influences. In that respect Japanese pluralism, with its genius for consensus formation, best represents the international dimension of East Asian civilization and, despite the great contrast in size between it and the United States, comes closest to our own outgoing impulse to incorporate new experience into a culture still in the process of formation.

I believe that we are entering a new and severely constricted phase of our development that will, contrary to the thrust of modern life so far, compel us to attend first to our inner space—of self-reflection, family intimacy, neighborly concern, and responsibility for our own bioregion—and only then to outer space. If I am right in this, we may have much to learn from both the Buddhist and the Neo-Confucian experience, especially from Chu Hsi's effort to define an educational curriculum aimed at the "shaping of a self"—"learning for the sake of one's self," as he put it—as a life formation on which a public philosophy could be grounded.

Chu's model for the curriculum—starting from a personal reading of and confrontation with the classics, followed by study of the major histories, and continuing as a lifelong discussion of value issues and contemporary problems, alongside the technical specialization for which Hu Yüan had recognized a need—is still worthy of consideration today. The "classics" would have to be more broadly representative of major world traditions; the "cosmology" should include what we now know about the larger universe and earth origins; the "history" would need to be extended to include biological and cultural evolution; and the "contemporary problems" would require updating, but in essence Chu's would still be a valid approach. As a pattern for a core curriculum balancing the specialized and vocational training so emphasized today, it would compare well with the requirements in effect at most colleges, and even better with those in many well-advertised institutions that trade heavily on the total flexibility of their approach to learning. Admittedly, however, such a program would have to go beyond the college years. Today a truly humane or liberal education can be conceived only as a lifelong enterprise, starting in the undergraduate years but continuing in graduate or professional school and adult education.

Chu recognized the compelling need for spiritual and moral training alongside the reading and discussion of books. Today we confront crises even more severe than his and threats far more deadly, implicit in the potential of new technologies for both catastrophic destruction and totalitarian control. No educational program will be able to meet these challenges that does not rouse the individual motivations and galvanize the human energies needed to cope with them—in other words, that does not by a virtual religious revolution reach deeply into the resources of the human spirit. Each of the four stages of civilization discussed here was inspired and sustained by such an inner revolution, while at the same time building upon the material and spiritual capital of the preceding age. This, I believe, will be no less true of the next great age of world civilization. No new order can endure that does not draw on the legacies of the past, but no tradition, whether Confucian, Buddhist, or Christian, can survive untransformed in the crucible of global struggle.

Often the study of East Asia is seen as one aspect of a larger program of international education that looks optimistically to new and expanded horizons, to consciousness raising, global awareness, and other grand visions of the future. But as we become more deeply conscious of the global dimensions of our problems, of our responsibility for the damage now being done to the earth, and of the jeopardy in which we have already put future generations, our education, instead of discussing universal values or the "humanities" in the abstract, will need to focus on something more concrete—on the best examples we can find of individual human beings, trying to meet their responsibilities in their own time, who have exercised their human freedom to make crucial decisions and difficult choices in facing such dilemmas. Trilling and Kolakowski worried about the erosion of any sense in modern culture that one can take responsibility for oneself and one's actions. I hope I have suggested here a few cases from the East Asian experience, now part of our common human inheritance, that can help us to recognize ourselves in such situations and suggest how we may begin to shape new selves more adequate to the prodigious challenges of both the present and the future.

Notes

Works Cited

Index

Notes

1. The Classical Age

1. Fung Yu-lan, "Response," in *Proceedings of the Heyman Center for the Humanities* (New York: Columbia University, 1982), p. 13.

2. *Analects* 1:1.

3. See *Analects* 9:25, where Confucius speaks of the inalienable autonomy of the common man: "The commander of great armies may be carried off, but the will of the common man cannot be taken from him," and 12:7, where he asserts that the most fundamental thing in government is mutual trust between rulers and ruled.

4. Tu Wei-ming, *Centrality and Commonality: An Essay on Chung Yung* (Honolulu: University of Hawaii Press, 1976), pp. 52–99.

5. Wang Hsien-ch'ien, *Hsun tzu chi-chieh* (Ch'angsha, 1891), 1:6a; translation, Burton Watson, *Hsün Tzu, Basic Writings* (New York: Columbia University Press, 1963), p. 18.

6. *Hsun tzu chi-chieh*, 1:8ab.

7. *Hsun tzu chi-chieh*, 1:8b; Watson, *Hsün Tzu*, p. 20.

8. *Hsun tzu chi-chieh*, 10a; Watson, *Hsün Tzu*, pp. 20–21.

9. *Hsun tzu chi-chieh*, 13a; adapted from Watson, *Hsün Tzu*, p. 23.

10. *Hsun tzu chi-chieh*, 13:1a.

11. A. L. Basham, *Studies in Indian History and Culture* (Calcutta: Sambodhi Publications, 1964), pp. 1–20.

12. Tung Chung-shu, *Ch'un-ch'iu fan-lu*, Ssu p'u ts'ung-k'an, 1st series, sec. 19 (Shanghai: Commercial Press, 1920-1922), 6:7a–8a; W. T. de Bary, Wing-tsit Chan, and Burton Watson, eds., *Sources of Chinese Tradition* (New York: Columbia University Press, 1960), I:162.

13. Pan Ku, *Han shu*, Pai-na-pen ed., 24A:14b–15b; de Bary, Chan, and Watson, *Sources of Chinese Tradition*, I:217.

14. Chen Huan-chang, *The Economic Principles of Confucius and His School* (New York: Columbia University Press, 1911), mentioned in

Derk Bodde, "Henry Wallace and the Ever-Normal Granary," *Far Eastern Quarterly* 5 (August 1946):411–426, reprinted in his *Essays on Chinese Civilization,* ed. Charles Le Blanc and Dorothy Borei (Princeton: Princeton University Press, 1981), pp. 18–20, 218–233.

2. *The Buddhist Age*

1. See de Bary, Chan, and Watson, *Sources of Chinese Tradition,* 1:274–279 (trans. Leon Hurwitz).

2. See Kenneth Ch'en, *The Chinese Transformation of Buddhism* (Princeton: Princeton University Press, 1973), pp. 105–106, 124.

3. The literature on the subject is vast. For our purposes it may suffice to note Edwin Reischauer's conclusion that the document "appears to represent Shōtoku's ideas." See E. O. Reischauer, J. K. Fairbank, and A. Craig, *East Asia: The Great Tradition* (Boston: Houghton Mifflin, 1958), p. 475; and Reischauer, *Japan: The Story of a Nation* (New York: Knopf, 1970), p. 20.

4. Konishi Jin'ichi, *A History of Japanese Literature* (Princeton: Princeton University Press, 1984), 1:311, concludes his weighing of the evidence, pro and con, with: "The Constitution may well be Shōtoku's work, but Korean immigrant intellectuals in his entourage must have also made major contributions. I would like to think that the solicitation of cooperation from these intellectuals, and the consolidation of a composition of such speculative force, could only have been effected if Prince Shōtoku himself was the author of the work." In any case, says Konishi, "we may conclude that the extant Constitution remains essentially a work of Suiko Tennō's time."

5. Justice Antonin Scalia, as quoted in the *New York Times,* Aug. 6, 1986, p. 13.

6. The text is collated and annotated by Ienaga Saburō and Tsukishima Hiroshi, *Shōtoku taishi shū,* in *Nihon shisō taikei* (Tokyo: Iwanami, 1976), 2:12–23; translation modified from W. G. Aston, *Nihongi, Chronicles of Japan* (London, Kegan Paul, 1930), 2:128–133.

7. *Shōtoku taishi shū,* p. 13.

8. *Shōtoku taishi shū,* p. 16.

9. Ibid., p. 18.

10. See the comments of Ienaga and Tsukishima, ibid., pp. 18, 383–384.

11. See Sakai Tadao, "Dissemination of Taoistic Religions over the Regions Surrounding China," *Proceedings of the 31st International Congress of Human Sciences in Asia and North Africa, 1983* (Tokyo: Tōhō gakkai, 1984), 2:246–274. Sakai rejects the earlier identification of *tennō* as a Taoist concept, identifying it with a distinct ritual tradition associated

with the gods of the T'ang capital, which of course served as the model for Japan's first settled capital at Nara. It was also during this period that the early histories were compiled.

12. *Shōtoku taishi shū*, p. 20.

13. Ibid., p. 20.

14. Ibid., p. 22.

15. Ibid., pp. 379–385.

16. Miyamoto Shōson, "The Relation of Philosophical Theory to Practical Affairs in Japan," in *The Japanese Mind*, ed. Charles A. Moore (Honolulu: University of Hawaii Press, 1967), p. 7.

17. D. L. Philippi, *Kojiki* (Tokyo: University of Tokyo Press, 1968), pp. 47–54, 81–86.

18. W. T. de Bary, ed., *The Buddhist Tradition* (New York: Random House, 1969), pp. 283–286, 309–313.

19. Carl Steenstrup, *Hōjō Shigetoki (1198–1261) and His Role in the History of Political and Ethical Ideas in Japan* (London: Curzon Press, 1979), pp. 167–168.

20. Philip Yampolsky, *The Platform Sutra of the Sixth Patriarch* (New York: Columbia University Press, 1967), pp. 126–127.

21. Yampolsky, *Platform Sutra*, pp. 127–128.

22. See Chun-fang Yü, "Chung-fen Ming-pen and Ch'an," in *Yüan Thought: Chinese Thought and Religion under the Mongols* ed. Hok-Lam Chan and W. T. de Bary (New York: Columbia University Press, 1982), pp. 431, 448–450.

23. Nien-ch'ang, *Fo-tsu li-tai t'ung-tsai*, in *Taishō shinshō daizōkyō*, 49:703c–704a, quoted by Jan Yün-hua, "Chinese Buddhism in Ta tu," in Chan and de Bary, *Yüan Thought*, p. 388.

24. Nien-ch'ang, *Taishō daizōkyō*, 49:704a.

3. The Neo-Confucian Age

1. Edwin O. Reischauer, *Ennin's Travels in T'ang China* (New York: Ronald Press, 1955), pp. 6–9.

2. See Y. Hervouet, ed., *A Sung Bibliography* (Hong Kong: Chinese University Press, 1978), pp. 319–320; S. Y. Teng and K. Biggerstaff, *An Annotated Bibliography of Selected Chinese Reference Works*, 3rd ed. (Cambridge, Mass.: Harvard University Press, 1971), p. 88; John Haeger, "The Significance of Confusion: The Origins of the T'ai-p'ing yu-lan," *Journal of the American Oriental Society* 88(3):401–410.

3. Haeger, in "Significance of Confusion," asserts that the *T'ai-p'ing yu-lan* did not actually see much use until after about 1030, by which time the demand for such reference works among officials and examination candidates had greatly increased.

4. See Erik Zürcher, "Buddhism and Education in T'ang Times," paper prepared for the Conference on Neo-Confucian Education: The Formative Stage, Princeton, N.J., September 1984.

5. Ch'eng Hao as quoted in Chu Hsi's *Chin-ssu lu*. See Mao Hsing-lai, *Chin-ssu lu chi-chu*, I-wen yin-shu-kuan reprint of Ssu-k'u shan-pen ed., 1st series (Taipei: Taiwan Commercial Press, 1978), 11:4b–5a; trans., Wing-tsit Chan, *Reflections on Things at Hand* (New York: Columbia University Press, 1967), pp. 262–263.

6. See Ho-nan Ch'eng-shih, *I-ch'üan wen-chi*, in *Erh Ch'eng ch'üan shu*, SPPY ed., 8:1. "Yen tzu so hao ho hsüeh lun." Translation by Wing-tsit Chan in *Source Book in Chinese Philosophy* (Princeton: Princeton University Press, 1963), pp. 547–550.

7. *Analects* 6:2, 9; 12:1. *Mencius* 4B:29.

8. See Liu Ts'un-yan, "Chu Hsi's Influence in Yüan Times," in *Chu Hsi and Neo-Confucianism,* ed. Wing-tsit Chan (Honolulu: University of Hawaii Press, 1985), p. 534, for a negative comment on this tendency in the Yüan.

9. de Bary, Chan, and Watson, *Sources of Chinese Tradition,* 1:393.

10. See A. F. Wright, *Buddhism in Chinese History* (Stanford: Stanford University Press, 1959), p. 983.

11. de Bary, *Buddhist Tradition,* pp. 68–70, 202–203.

12. See the comments included, with the obvious approval of Chu Hsi, in the *Chin-ssu lu,* chap. 13; Mao Hsing-lai, *Chin ssu-lu chi-chu,* 13:1a–9b; Chan, *Reflections on Things at Hand,* pp. 280–285. See also de Bary, Chan, and Watson, *Sources of Chinese Tradition,* pp. 477–478.

13. See Thomas H. C. Lee, *Government Education and Examinations in Sung China* (Hong Kong: Chinese University Press, 1985), pp. 66–67, 107–108, 119–124, 247–249.

14. Chu Hsi, *Hui-an hsien-sheng Chu Wen-kung wen-chi* (Kyoto: Chūbun shuppansha, 1977), 70:9a (p. 1279). Tu liang Ch'en chien-i i-mo.

15. See W. T. de Bary, *The Liberal Tradition in China* (Hong Kong: Chinese University Press, 1983), pp. 32–34.

16. Li Ching-te, comp., *Chu Tzu yü-lei* (Taipei: Cheng-chung shu-chü, 1970), 126:7b (4830), 10a (4835), and esp. 13a (4841). See also Okada Takehiko, "Practical Learning in the Chu Hsi School," in *Principle and Practicality,* ed. W. T. de Bary and Irene Bloom (New York: Columbia University Press, 1979), pp. 240–241.

17. Chu, *Wen-chi,* 1:21ab (pp. 261–262) Chiu Yü chai . . . , Tu men; Tomoeda Ryutarō, *Shushi no shisō keisei,* rev. ed. (Tokyo: Shunjusha, 1979), pp. 41–51.

18. *Liberal Tradition,* pp. 21–24.

19. Chu Hsi, *Ta-hsüeh chang-chu* (Taipei: Chung-kuo ming-chu chi-ch'eng, 1978), 6ab (pp. 17–18).

20. I discuss this point more fully in "Neo-Confucian Individualism

and Holism," in *Individualism and Holism: Studies in Confucian and Taoist Values,* ed. Donald Munro (Ann Arbor: University of Michigan Press, 1985), pp. 351–358.

21. Chu, *Ta-hsüeh chang-chu,* preface, 3b (p. 6), 13b (p. 32).

22. de Bary, *Liberal Tradition,* pp. 28, 37–40, 52–57; Martina Deuchler, "Self-Cultivation for the Governance of Men," *Asiatische Studien* 34 (1980):16.

23. Chu Hsi, *Chung-yung chang-chü,* in *Ssu-shu chi-chu* (Taipei: Chung-kuo tzu-hsüeh ming-chu chi-ch'eng, 1978), 1a–2b (pp. 37–40).

24. See Benjamin Elman, "Philosophy (I-li) versus Philology (K'ao-cheng): The *jen-hsin tao-hsin* Debate," *T'oung Pao* 69, (1983), 175–222.

25. *Chung-yung chang-chü,* preface, 1b (p. 38).

26. Ibid., 1a (p. 45). *Erh-ch'eng ch'üan-shu,* SPPY ed., Wai-shu, 11:1b.

27. The process of extraction had already been begun by Chu's predecessors in the Sung, but he gave it authoritative confirmation. See my *Neo-Confucian Orthodoxy and the Learning of the Mind and Heart* (New York: Columbia University Press, 1981), pp. 91–92.

28. de Bary, *Neo-Confucian Orthodoxy,* pp. 129, 189, 211; and W. T. de Bary and Ja-Hyun Kim Haboush, *The Rise of Neo-Confucianism in Korea* (New York: Columbia University Press, 1985).

29. See Gari K. Ledyard, *The Korean Language Reform of 1446: The Origin, Background and Early History of the Korean Alphabet* (Ann Arbor: University Microfilms, 1966), pp. 151–165, 221–260.

30. See de Bary and Bloom, *Principle and Practicality,* esp. pp. 19–29, 257–290.

31. See Martina Deuchler, "Reject the False and Uphold the Straight: Attitudes towards Heterodox Thought in Early Yi Korea," in W. T. de Bary and Ja-Hyun Kim Haboush, eds., *The Rise of Neo-Confucianism in Korea* (New York: Columbia University Press, 1985), pp. 400–404.

32. See de Bary, *Sources of Chinese Tradition,* p. 597.

33. An excellent illustration of this trend is given in Lynn Struve, "The Early Ch'ing Legacy of Huang Tsung-hsi: A Reexamination," *Asia Major,* forthcoming, showing what became of even the relatively independent scholarship produced in the intellectual lineage from Wang Yang-ming to Huang Tsung-hsi and Ch'üan Tsu-wang. See also Benjamin Elman, *From Philosophy to Philology* (Cambridge, Mass.: Harvard University Press, 1984), pp. 231–247, 254.

4. East Asia's Modern Transformation

1. Excerpted from S. Y. Teng and J. K. Fairbank, *China's Response to the West: a Documentary Survey, 1839–1923* (Cambridge, Mass.: Harvard University Press, 1954), pp. 24–25.

2. See Mark Elvin, *The Pattern of the Chinese Past* (Stanford: Stanford University Press, 1973), pp. 215–221; de Bary, *Neo-Confucian Orthodoxy*, pp. 24–27, 36–60; Chan and de Bary, *Yüan Thought*, pp. 2–4.

3. See L. C. Goodrich and C. Fang, eds., *Dictionary of Ming Biography* (New York: Columbia University Press, 1976), p. 197, and Wang Gung-wu's account of Hsia Yüan-chi, pp. 532–533.

4. See Ronald P. Toby, *State and Diplomacy in Early Modern Japan* (Princeton: Princeton University Press, 1984), pp. 46–64, 80–81, 96, 170–173, 244–246.

5. See Burton Watson, trans., *The Complete Works of Chuang Tzu* (New York: Columbia University Press, 1968), pp. 30–31.

6. Wang Hsien-ch'ien, *Chuang-tzu chi-chieh* (Shanghai: Commercial Press, Kuo-hsüeh chi-pen tsung-shu ed., 7/49); translation adapted from E. R. Hughes, *Chinese Philosophy in Classical Times* (London: Dent, 1942), p. 199.

7. Teng and Fairbank, *China's Response to the West*, pp. 24–27; de Bary, Chan, and Watson, *Sources of Chinese Tradition*, 666–668.

8. Teng and Fairbank, *China's Response to the West*, pp. 28–36; de Bary, Chan, and Watson, *Sources of Chinese Tradition*, 672–679.

9. Among the many works that might be cited, one that deals most specifically with the transition from the attitude of expelling the barbarian (*jōi*) to the policy of opening the country (*kaikoku*) is Conrad Totman, "From Sakoku to Kaikoku: The Transformation of Foreign Policy Attitudes, 1853–68," *Monumenta Nipponica* 35 (1980):1–20.

10. See R. Tsunoda, W. T. de Bary, and Donald Keene, *Sources of Japanese Tradition* (New York: Columbia University Press, 1958), pp. 616–622, 638–646.

11. Hirose Yutaka, *Yoshida Shōin no kenkyū* (Tokyo, Musashino shoin, 1930), pp. 197–220, 253–285; Oyanagi Shigeta, *Zoku Tōyōshi no kenkyū* (Tokyo: Morikita shoten, 1943), pp. 179–180.

12. Oyanagi, *Zoku Tōyōshi*; Maruyama Masao, *Studies in the Intellectual History of Tokugawa Japan* (Tokyo: Tokyo University Press), 1974, pp. 206–222.

13. R. L. Stevenson, "Yoshida Torajirō," reprinted in *Yoshida Shōin zenshū*, ed. Hirose Yutaka (Tokyo: Iwanami, 1935), 10:864, 868.

14. *Yoshida Shōin zenshū*, 4:281–282, letter, Jan. 23, 1859, to his younger sister; 6:361–363, letter, July 1859, to Takasugi Shinsaku; 8:544–546, Dokuyo zassho 9, Winter 1858–59, Rishi funsho; Kawakami Tetsutarō, *Yoshida Shōin: Bu to ju ni yoru ningenzō* (Tokyo: Chuko bunko, 1979), pp. 234–249; Hirose, *Yoshida Shōin no kenkyū*, pp. 8, 180–185, 256–268, 366–368. "Mad ardor" is Julia Ching's translation of the Chinese *k'uang chuan*, much admired by Shōin.

15. Based on conversations with his wife Mishima Yoko and the

journalist Tokuoka Takao and on Donald Keene's conversations with Mishima. Mishima's views on the Wang Yang-ming teaching as a source of revolutionary thought in the Bakumatsu-Meiji period are found in his novel *Homba* (Runaway Horses) and in his essay "Kakumei Tetsugaku toshite no Yōmeigaku," in *Mishima Yukio Zenshū* (Tokyo: Shinchōsha, 1976), 34:449–482 (first published in the magazine *Shokun,* September 1970). Uno Seiichi is reported to have lectured on "Yōmeigaku to Mishima Yukio," Apr. 25, 1973, as the Twenty-Second Memorial Lecture sponsored by the Mishima Yukio Research Society, but the text is not available in print. It remains an open question as to how well Mishima understood Wang Yang-ming.

16. Okada Takehiko, "Neo-Confucian Thinkers in Nineteenth Century Japan," in *Confucianism and Tokugawa Culture,* ed. Peter Nosco (Princeton: Princeton University Press, 1984), pp. 215–250. The point, of course, is not new. See Oyanagi, *Zoku Tōyōshi,* pp. 109–189.

17. Oyanagi, *Zoku Tōyōshi,* 187–188, sees this formulation as the basic rationale for the new education of the Meiji period.

18. Tsunoda, de Bary, and Keene, *Sources of Japanese Tradition,* pp. 643–644.

19. Marius Jansen, *The Japanese and Sun Yat-sen* (Cambridge, Mass.: Harvard University Press, 1954), p. 18.

20. Teng and Fairbank, *China's Response to the West,* p. 50; de Bary, Chan, and Watson, *Sources of Chinese Tradition,* pp. 707–721.

21. See, for instance, those cited by Benjamin Schwartz, *In Search of Wealth and Power: Yen Fu and the West* (Cambridge, Mass.: Harvard University Press, 1964), pp. 8–9.

22. Teng and Fairbank, *China's Response to the West,* p. 76.

23. See my *Neo-Confucian Orthodoxy,* p. 59, and "Chu Hsi's Aims in Education," in *Neo-Confucian Education: The Formative Stage,* ed. W. T. de Bary and John Chaffee (Berkeley: University of California Press, 1988).

24. Chang Tsai, *Chang Tzu ch'üan-shu* (Kyoto: Chūbun shuppansha Kinsei kanseki sōkan ed., 1972), 2c:20a (p. 439, Cheng-meng 7); *Chin-ssu lu chi-chu* 2:37a; translation, Chan, *Reflections on Things at Hand,* p. 84.

25. Chang Tsai, *Chang Tzu ch'üan-shu* 14:15b; *Chin-ssu lu chi-chu* 2:49b; translation, Chan, *Reflections on Things at Hand,* pp. 74–75. It is true that the concepts of the mind and of learning in this and the preceding quotation do not exactly correspond to modern conceptions, but in the context of the *Chin-ssu lu* there would be no doubt that both intellectual inquiry and an empathetic openness to others was being encouraged.

26. Schwartz, *Wealth and Power,* p. 18.

27. Ibid., p. 17.

28. Chang Po-hsing, Personal Preface to the Ch'eng-shih . . . jih-

ch'eng, *Cheng-i t'ang ch'üan-shu* (Fu-chou Cheng-i hsüeh yüan ed. of 1868), 1:1.

29. Among these, perhaps the most pertinent are Evelyn Rawski, *Education and Popular Literacy in Ch'ing China* (Ann Arbor: University of Michigan Press, 1979); David Johnson, Andrew Nathan, and Evelyn Rawski, eds., *Popular Culture in Late Imperial China* (Berkeley: University of California Press, 1985); and Thomas H. C. Lee, *Government Education and Examinations in Sung China* (Hong Kong: Chinese University Press, 1985).

30. Ch'en Chien, *Hsüeh-pu t'ung-pien* (reprint, Taipei: Kuang-wen 1971), personal preface, p. 1; also Morohashi Tetsuji et al., eds., *Shushigaku taikei* (Tokyo: Meitoku, 1974), 10:532 (Japanese trans., p. 369).

31. *Hsüeh-pu t'ung-pien*, T'i-kang, p. 2. *Shushigaku taikei*, 10:533b (373).

32. Schwartz, *Wealth and Power*, pp. 17–19.

33. Hsiao Kung-ch'üan, *A Modern China and a New World: K'ang Yu-wei, Reformer and Utopian, 1858–1927* (Seattle: University of Washington Press, 1975) pp. 21–31.

34. Hsiao, *A Modern China*, pp. 59–60.

35. *K'ang Nan-hai tzu-pien nien-p'u*, in *Wu-hsü pien-fa*, Comp. Chien Po-tsan et al. (Shanghai, 1953), 4:117; translation by Richard C. Howard in "K'ang Yu-wei (1858–1927): His Intellectual Background and Early Thought," in *Confucian Personalities*, ed. A. Wright and D. Twitchett (Stanford University Press, 1962), p. 301.

36. See Jen Yu-wen, "Ch'en Hsien-chang's Philosophy of the Natural," in *Self and Society in Ming Thought*, ed. W. T. de Bary (New York: Columbia University Press, 1970), pp. 53–86; and my "Individualism and Humanitarianism in Late Ming Thought," ibid., pp. 157–169.

37. See my *Neo-Confucian Orthodoxy*, pp. 9–13; and *Liberal Tradition in China*, pp. 11–20.

38. This is the subject of an extensive study I have made of Lü's thought in connection with a forthcoming work on individualism in Neo-Confucian thought. I gave a preliminary report, titled "Lü Liu-liang (1629–1683) and the Return to Orthodoxy," to the University Seminar on Traditional China, Columbia University, October 1985.

39. Hsiao, *A Modern China*, pp. 380–381.

40. A striking illustration of how this operated in the Neo-Confucian mind is found in Chang Po-hsing's preface to his Compilation for Nurturing Correctness (*Yang cheng lei-pien*), in *Cheng-i t'ang ch'üan-shu*, vol. 1a–2b). As both a high official and a leading exponent of Chu Hsi orthodoxy, Chang was critical of the deleterious effects of the examination system on education and worked tirelessly to "nourish correctness," that is, to inculcate the true teaching in its purity and correct practice. Explaining how this

"correctness" should extend to Heaven-and-Earth and all things, through the agency of the sages and worthies, he says that "when this reaches the myriad peoples, they will all participate in the settlements of farmer-soldiers (*t'un-t'ien*), whereby they would plough the fields and garrison the land, so that the foundation of society would be correctly and firmly established." To the best of my knowledge Chu Hsi himself never attached such fundamental importance to the *t'un-t'ien,* but the latter could be considered quite congenial to Chu's general emphasis on local self-sufficiency and communality as the essential basis of the polity, following the pattern set at the top by the ruler's supposedly wise and unselfish example.

41. See John E. Schrecker, "The Reform Movement of 1898," in *Reform in Nineteenth Century China,* ed. Paul A. Cohen and John E. Schrecker (Cambridge, Mass.: Harvard University Press, 1976), pp. 293–295.

42. Jansen, *Japanese and Sun Yat-sen,* pp. 75–77.

43. Hsiao, *A Modern China,* p. 384.

44. K. C. Chang, *Art, Myth, and Ritual,* (Cambridge, Mass.: Harvard University Press, 1983), pp. 88–89.

45. de Bary, *Liberal Tradition in China,* chap. 1.

46. Lü Liu-liang, *Ssu-shu chiang-i* (43-chapter ed. of 1686), 6:10ab; 17:9a; 37:1b–2a; 38:8ab; W. T. de Bary, "Chinese Despotism and the Confucian Ideal," in *Chinese Thought and Institutions,* ed. J. K. Fairbank (Chicago: University of Chicago Press, 1957), pp. 163–203.

47. K'ang Yu-wei *Lun-yü chu* (Wan-mu ts'ao-t'ang ts'ung-shu ed., 20 chapters, 1917), 2:11ab.

48. Sun Yat-sen, *Chung-shan ch'üan-shu,* 4 vols. (Shanghai: San min tu-shu kung-ssu, 1946), 1:4–5.

49. Ibid., pp. 15–16, 28–29, 51–52.

50. Teng and Fairbank, *China's Response to the West,* pp. 246–249.

51. Mao Tse-tung, *Selected Works* (London: Lawrence and Wishart, 1954), 1:56.

52. Mao, *Selected Works,* 2:74–76.

53. Liu Shao-ch'i, *How to Be a Good Communist* (New York: New Century, 1952), pp. 15–16.

5. The Post-Confucian Era

1. de Bary, *Neo-Confucian Orthodoxy,* pp. ix–x.

2. Chong Won-shik, "Zeal for Education," *Korea Journal,* 26 (October 1986):47–48.

3. See, for a recent example, Kurt Dopfer, "Ideas as Determinants of Socio-Economic Development: Asian Concepts of the Proper Way," Diskussions beiträge no. 40, Forschungs gemeinschaft für National ökonomie

an der Hochschule, St. Gallen, April 1985. Dopfer considers the Japanese Way, based primarily on Shinto beliefs, aided by a pragmatic Buddhism, to have been more conducive to change than a "conservative," "closed" Confucianism, which blocked China's modernization. Quite apart from the adequacy of his characterization of the thought systems involved, the argument is closely tied to a contrast between China and Japan in nation-building efforts. After World War II the influence of Confucianism, or the lack of anything compared to Shinto, have certainly not held back Korea, Taiwan, Hong Kong, or Singapore.

4. *New York Times,* Sept. 28, 1986, p. 56.

5. See Sakai Tadao, "Yi Yulgok and the Community Compact," in *The Rise of Neo-Confucianism in Korea,* ed. W. T. de Bary and Ja-Hyun Kim Haboush (New York: Columbia University Press, 1985), pp. 323–344, esp. p. 326.

6. *Analects* II, 21.

7. Ibid., II, 4.

6. East Asia and the West

1. Here I am drawing in part on my response to Paul Cohen's review of *The Liberal Tradition in China.* His review appeared under the title "The Quest of Liberalism in the Chinese Past" in *Philosophy East and West,* 35 (July 1985):305–310. My reply, ibid. (October 1985): 399–412, was entitled: "Confucian Liberalism and Western Parochialisms." Professor Cohen's response to it is in the same issue, pp. 413–417.

2. Jack Kirwan, "Mandarin Mondale and U.S. Future in Space," *Wall Street Journal,* Oct. 23, 1984.

3. Ibid.

4. Arthur Waley, *Monkey* (London: George Allen and Unwin, 1942), p. 75.

5. Ibid., pp. 75–76.

6. Lionel Trilling, "The Uncertain Future of Humanistic Education," *American Scholar* (Winter 1974–75): 56–57.

7. Leszek Kolakowski, "The Idolatry of Politics," *New Republic,* June 16, 1986.

8. Ibid. In saying that Confucians would probably not accept any dichotomy between the moral and biological, I should acknowledge that Kolakowski's real point is more to affirm the moral reality than to set up any antithesis between the two.

Works Cited

Aston, W. G., trans. *Nihongi, Chronicles of Japan*, vol. 2. London: Kegan Paul, 1930.

Basham, A. L. *Studies in Indian History and Culture*. Calcutta: Sambodhi Publications, 1964.

Bodde, Derk. "Henry Wallace and the Ever-Normal Granary." *Far Eastern Quarterly* 5 (August 1946):411–426; reprinted in *Essays on Chinese Civilization*, ed. Charles Le Blanc and Dorothy Borei. Princeton: Princeton University Press, 1981.

Chan, Wing-tsit. *Reflections on Things at Hand*. New York: Columbia University Press, 1967.

———. *Source-Book in Chinese Philosophy*. Princeton: Princeton University Press, 1963.

Chang, K. C. *Art, Myth, and Ritual*. Cambridge, Mass.: Harvard University Press, 1983.

Chang Po-hsing. *Cheng-i t'ang ch'üan-shu*. Fu-chou Cheng-i hsüeh yüan ed. of 1868.

Chang Tsai. *Chang Tzu ch'üan-shu*. Kyoto: Chūbun shuppansha. Kinsei kanseki sōkan ed., Shisō hen vols. 2, 3. Taipei: Kuang-wen shu-chü, 1979.

Ch'en, Kenneth. *The Chinese Transformation of Buddhism*. Princeton: Princeton University Press, 1973.

Ch'en Chien. *Hsüeh-pu t'ung-pien*. Reprint, Taipei: Kuang-wen, 1971.

Chen Huan-chang. *The Economic Principles of Confucius and His School*. New York: Columbia University Press, 1911.

Chien Po-tsan, et al., comps. *Wu-hsü pien-fa*. Shanghai, 1953.

Chong Won-shik. "Zeal for Education." *Korea Journal* 26 (October 1986):47–48.

Chu Hsi. *Hui-an hsien-sheng Chu Wen-kung wen-chi*. Kyoto: Chūbun shuppansha, 1977.

———. *Chung-yung chang-chü.* In *Ssu-shu chi-chu.* Chung-kuo tzu-hsüeh ming-chu chi-ch'eng. Taipei, 1978.

———. *Ta-hsüeh chang-chü.* Chung-kuo ming-chu chi-ch'eng ed. Taipei, 1978.

Cohen, Paul. "The Quest for Liberalism in the Chinese Past." *Philosophy East and West* 35 (July 1985):305–310.

Confucius. *Analects.* In *The Chinese Classics,* vol. 1, trans. James Legge. Oxford: Clarendon Press, 1893.

———. *Mencius.* In *The Chinese Classics,* vol. 1, trans. James Legge. Oxford: Clarendon Press, 1893.

de Bary, W. T. "Chinese Despotism and the Confucian Ideal." In *Chinese Thought and Institutions,* ed. J. K. Fairbank. Chicago: University of Chicago Press, 1957.

———. *The Buddhist Tradition.* New York: Random House, 1969.

———. *Neo-Confucian Orthodoxy and the Learning of the Mind and Heart.* New York: Columbia University Press, 1981.

———. *The Liberal Tradition in China.* Hong Kong: Chinese University Press, 1983.

———. "Neo-Confucian Individualism and Holism." In *Individualism and Holism: Studies in Confucian and Taoist Values,* ed. Donald Munro. Ann Arbor: University of Michigan Press, 1985.

———. "Lü Liu-liang (1629–1683) and the Return to Orthodoxy." Paper delivered to the University Seminar on Traditional China, Columbia University, October 1985.

———. "Confucian Liberalism and Western Parochialisms." *Philosophy East and West* 35 (October 1985):399–412.

de Bary, W. T., and Irene Bloom, eds. *Principle and Practicality.* New York: Columbia University Press, 1979.

de Bary, W. T., and John Chaffee, eds. *Neo-Confucian Education: The Formative Stage.* Berkeley: University of California Press, 1987.

de Bary, W. T., Wing-tsit Chan, and Burton Watson, eds. *Sources of Chinese Tradition,* vols. 1 and 2. New York: Columbia University Press, 1960.

de Bary, W. T., and Ja-Hyun Kim Haboush, eds. *The Rise of Neo-Confucianism in Korea.* New York: Columbia University Press, 1985.

Deuchler, Martina. "Self-Cultivation for the Governance of Men." *Asiatische Studien* 34 (1980): 9–39.

———. "Reject the False and Uphold the Straight: Attitudes towards Heterodox Thought in Early Yi Korea." In *The Rise of Neo-Confucianism in Korea,* ed. W. T. de Bary and Ja-Hyun Kim Haboush. New York: Columbia University Press, 1985.

Dopfer, Kurt. "Ideas as Determinants of Socio-Economic Development: Asian Concepts of the Proper Way." Diskussions beiträge no. 40,

Forschungs gemeinschaft für National ökonomie an der Hochschule, St. Gallen, April 1985.

Elman, Benjamin. "Philosophy (I-li) versus Philology (K'ao-cheng): The *jen-hsin tao-hsin* Debate." *T'oung Pao* 69 (1983):175–222.

———. *From Philosophy to Philology.* Cambridge, Mass.: Harvard University Press, 1984.

Elvin, Mark. *The Pattern of the Chinese Past.* Stanford: Stanford University Press, 1973.

Erh Ch'eng ch'üan-shu. SPPY ed., comp. Hsü Pi-ta.

Fung Yu-lan. "Response." In *Proceedings of the Heyman Center for the Humanities.* New York, 1982.

Goodrich, L. C., and C. Fang, eds. *Dictionary of Ming Biography.* New York: Columbia University Press, 1976.

Haeger, John. "The Significance of Confusion: The Origins of the T'aip'ing yu-lan." *Journal of the American Oriental Society* 88 (3):401–410.

Hervouet, Y., ed. *A Sung Bibliography.* Hong Kong: Chinese University Press, 1978.

Hirose Yutaka. *Yoshida Shōin no kenkyū.* Tokyo: Musashino shoin, 1930.

Howard, Richard C. "K'ang Yu-wei (1858–1927): His Intellectual Background and Early Thought." In *Confucian Personalities,* ed. A. Wright and D. Twitchett. Stanford: Stanford University Press, 1962.

Hsiao Kung-ch'üan. *A Modern China and a New World: K'ang Yu-wei, Reformer and Utopian, 1858–1927.* Seattle: University of Washington Press, 1975.

Hughes, E. R. *Chinese Philosophy in Classical Times.* London: Dent, 1942.

Ienaga Saburō and Tsukishima Hiroshi, eds. *Shōtoku taishi shū,* in *Nihōn shisō taikei,* vol. 2. Tokyo: Iwanami, 1976.

Jan, Yün-hua. "Chinese Buddhism in Ta-tu." In *Yüan Thought: Chinese Thought and Religion under the Mongols,* ed. Hok-Lam Chan and W. T. de Bary. New York: Columbia University Press, 1982.

Jansen, Marius. *The Japanese and Sun Yat-sen.* Cambridge, Mass.: Harvard University Press, 1954.

Jen Yu-wen. "Ch'en Hsien-chang's Philosophy of the Natural." In *Self and Society in Ming Thought,* ed. W. T. de Bary. New York: Columbia University Press, 1970.

Johnson, David, Andrew Nathan, and Evelyn Rawski, eds. *Popular Culture in Late Imperial China.* Berkeley: University of California Press, 1985.

K'ang Yu-wei. *Lun-yü chu.* Wan-mu ts'ao-t'ang ts'ung-shu ed., 20 chapters, 1917.

Kawakami Tetsutarō. *Yoshida Shōin: Bu to ju ni yoru ningenzō.* Tokyo: Chuko Bunko, 1979.

Kirwan, Jack. "Mandarin Mondale and U.S. Future in Space." *Wall Street Journal,* Oct. 23, 1984.

Kolakowski, Leszek. "The Idolatry of Politics." *New Republic,* June 16, 1986.

Konishi Jin'ichi. *A History of Japanese Literature.* Princeton: Princeton University Press, 1984.

Ledyard, Gari K. *The Korean Language Reform of 1446: The Origin, Background and Early History of the Korean Alphabet.* Ann Arbor: University Microfilms, 1966.

Lee, Thomas H. C. *Government Education and Examinations in Sung China.* Hong Kong: Chinese University Press, 1985.

Li Ching-te, comp. *Chu Tzu yü-lei.* Taipei: Cheng-chung shu-chü, 1970.

Liu Shao-ch'i. *How to Be a Good Communist.* New York: New Century, 1952.

Liu Ts'un-yan. "Chu Hsi's Influence in Yüan Times." In *Chu Hsi and Neo-Confucianism,* ed. Wing-tsit Chan. Honolulu: University of Hawaii Press, 1985.

Lü Liu-liang. *Ssu-shu chiang-i.* 43–chapter ed. of 1686.

Mao Hsing-lai. *Chin-ssu lu chi-chu.* Ssu-k'u shan-pen ts'ung-shu, 1st series. Taipei: Taiwan Commercial Press, 1978.

Mao Tse-tung. *Selected Works.* London: Lawrence and Wishart, 1954.

Maruyama Masao. *Studies in the Intellectual History of the Tokugawa Period.* Tokyo: Tokyo University Press, 1974.

Mishima Yukio. *Mishima Yukio Zenshū.* Tokyo: Shinchōsha, 1976.

Miyamoto Shōson. "The Relation of Philosophical Theory to Practical Affairs in Japan." In *The Japanese Mind,* ed. Charles A. Moore. Honolulu: University of Hawaii Press, 1967.

Morohashi Tetsuji et al., eds. *Shushigaku taikei.* Tokyo: Meitoku shuppansha, 1974.

Nien-ch'ang. *Fo tsu li-tai t'ung-tsai.* In *Taishō shinshū daizōkyō,* vol. 49. Tokyo, 1914–1922.

Okada Takehiko. "Neo-Confucian Thinkers in Nineteenth Century Japan." In *Confucianism and Tokugawa Culture,* ed. Peter Nosco. Princeton: Princeton University Press, 1984.

Oyanagi Shigeta. *Zoku Tōyōshi no kenkyū.* Tokyo: Morikita shoten, 1943.

Pan Ku. *Han shu.* Pai-na-pen ed.

Philippi, D. L., trans. *Kojiki.* Tokyo: University of Tokyo Press, 1968.

Rawski, Evelyn. *Education and Popular Literacy in Ch'ing China.* Ann Arbor: University of Michigan Press, 1979.

Reischauer, Edwin O. *Ennin's Travels in T'ang China.* New York: Ronald Press, 1955.

————. *Japan, The Story of a Nation.* New York: Alfred A. Knopf, 1970.

Reischauer, E. O., J. K. Fairbank, and A. Craig. *East Asia: The Great Tradition.* Boston: Houghton Mifflin, 1959.

Sakai Tadao. "Dissemination of Taoistic Religions over the Regions Surrounding China." *Proceedings of the 31st International Congress of Human Sciences in Asia and North Africa, 1983,* vol. 2. Tokyo: Tōhō gakkai, 1984.

————. "Yi Yulgok and the Community Compact." In *The Rise of Neo-Confucianism in Korea,* ed. W. T. de Bary and Ja-Hyun Kim Haboush. New York: Columbia University Press, 1985.

Schrecker, John E. "The Reform Movement of 1898." In *Reform in Nineteenth Century China,* ed. Paul A. Cohen and John E. Schrecker. Cambridge, Mass.: Harvard University Press, 1976.

Schwartz, Benjamin. *In Search of Wealth and Power: Yen Fu and the West.* Cambridge, Mass.: Harvard University Press, 1964.

Steenstrup, Carl. *Hōjō Shigetoki (1198–1261) and His Role in the History of Political and Ethical Ideas in Japan.* London: Curzon Press, 1979.

Stevenson, R. L. "Yoshida Torajirō." Reprinted in *Yoshida Shōin zenshū,* ed. Hirose Yutaka. Tokyo: Iwanami, 1935.

Struve, Lynn. "The Early Ch'ing Legacy of Huang Tsung-hsi: A Reexamination." *Asia Major,* 3rd series, vol. 1 (Fall 1987).

Sun Yat-sen. *Chung-shan ch'üan-shu,* 4 vols. Shanghai: San min tu-shu kung-ssu, 1946.

Teng, S. Y., and K. Biggerstaff. *An Annotated Bibliography of Chinese Reference Works,* 3rd ed. Cambridge, Mass.: Harvard University Press, 1971.

Teng, S. Y., and J. K. Fairbank. *China's Response to the West: A Documentary Survey, 1839–1923.* Cambridge, Mass.: Harvard University Press, 1954.

Toby, Ronald P. *State and Diplomacy in Early Modern Japan.* Princeton: Princeton University Press, 1984.

Tomoeda Ryūtarō. *Shushi no shisō keisei,* rev. ed. Tokyo: Shunjusha, 1979.

Totman, Conrad. "From Sakoku to Kaikoku: The Transformation of Foreign Policy Attitudes, 1853–68." *Monumenta Nipponica* 35 (1980):1–20.

Trilling, Lionel. "The Uncertain Future of Humanistic Education." *American Scholar* (Winter 1974–75):56–57.

Tsunoda, R., W. T. de Bary, and Donald Keene. *Sources of Japanese Tradition.* New York: Columbia University Press, 1958.

Tung Chung-shu. *Ch'un-ch'iu fan-lu.* Ssu-p'u ts'ung-k'an, 1st series, sec. 19. Shanghai: Commercial Press, 1920–1922.

Tu Wei-ming. *Centrality and Commonality: An Essay in Chung Yung.* Honolulu: University of Hawaii Press, 1976.

Waley, Arthur. *Monkey.* London: George Allen and Unwin, 1942.

Wang Hsien-ch'ien. *Chuang-tzu chi-chieh,* Kuo-hsüeh chi-pen ts'ung-shu ed. Commercial Press.

———. *Hsun tzu chi-chieh.* Ch'angsha, 1891.

Watson, Burton, trans. *Hsün Tzu, Basic Writings.* New York: Columbia University Press, 1963.

———. *The Complete Works of Chuang Tzu.* New York: Columbia University Press, 1968.

Wright, A. F. *Buddhism in Chinese History.* Stanford: Stanford University Press, 1959.

Yampolsky, Philip, trans. *The Platform Sutra of the Sixth Patriarch.* New York: Columbia University Press, 1967.

Yü, Chun-fang. "Chung-fen Ming-pen and Ch'an." In *Yüan Thought: Chinese Thought and Religion under the Mongols,* ed. Hok-Lam Chan and W. T. de Bary. New York: Columbia University Press, 1982.

Zürcher, Erik. "Buddhism and Education in T'ang Times." Paper prepared for the Conference on Neo-Confucian Education: The Formative Stage, Princeton, N.J., September 1984.

Index